US
101
A HIGHWAY ADVENTURE

Best Regards
Earl Roberge A.S.M.P.

The birds of the air,
The fish of the sea,
The mountains, the plains
and whatever will be
That passes along the road,
the road by the sea.

The Book of Psalms

US 101
A HIGHWAY ADVENTURE

Photography and Text by
EARL ROBERGE

Foreword by
ROBERT MONDAVI

Beautiful America Publishing Company
T.M.

International Standard Book Number 0-89802-547-8
Library of Congress Catalog Card Number 90-30963
Copyright© 1990 by
Beautiful America Publishing Company©
P.O. Box 646, Wilsonville, Oregon 97070 (503) 682-0173

Design & Production: Michael Brugman
Typographer: Oregon Typesetting
Printed in Hong Kong

DEDICATION

To Millie Roberge Gordon,
loving and dutiful daughter
who brought to fruition
the idea that the adventure
of US 101 should be shared,
this book is lovingly dedicated.

TABLE OF CONTENTS

TABLE OF CONTENTS

ACKNOWLEDGMENTS

If you were to ask the creator of a beautiful garden just when the beauty spread out before our eyes was created, the answer probably would be a puzzled look and a bemused "I don't really know," because the evolution of a garden is a gradual thing; the culmination of years of dreaming turned into effort, and it is difficult to assign a specific date to its beginning.

So it is with this book. In searching my memory for the exact time that the seed that blossomed into this work was planted, I must go way back to 1945, and my first experience with Highway 101, because whether or not I realized it at that time, that probably was when the idea that this fascinating experience should somehow be shared with others first took root. It may have been a forgotten seed, planted way back there in the far recesses of a mind much more preoccupied with the mundane problems of making a living and carving out a niche in life, but it was there, and needed only the right time, place, and encouragement to bring it into the light of day.

Another thought comes immediately to mind: it takes the concerted help of a lot of people to turn any idea into the wonderfully complex entity of paper, colored ink, and photographs that is a modern pictorial book. Without the help of literally hundreds of skilled technicians, the seed that was planted so long ago might have withered and died, and even if it had flourished in my mind, would have been destined to die unseen.

Good manners as well as simple justice demand that proper thanks be given to those who have given me a helping hand along the way, and those technicians are certainly high on that list; but there are many others without whose help and encouragement this book would still be an unfulfilled dream.

It also is a reality that I could be opening a barrel of snakes here, for the number of people who have helped me along the way numbers into the hundreds, and if I inadvertently should not mention someone who should be, I would be hurting a friend who deserves better. Simply to cover myself, please feel included in the blanket but nevertheless very sincere "Thank You" I hereby tender to anyone who in even the smallest degree helped me compile the story of Highway 101.

Of all those "thank you"'s the most sincere and heartfelt rightfully goes to Millie Roberge Gordon, my loving daughter who finally convinced her Daddy that he should find a publisher for the 101 book, because she, too, had for years felt that this was a fitting subject for a large pictorial book, and thought that this would be a fitting canvas on which the many good photos she knew I had of this road could be displayed. She has always been able to twist me around her little finger, and this time was no exception. My thanks to you, Honey, for convincing me that this monumental task was within the capabilities of your old Dad, and for all the helpful suggestions and ideas your fertile brain conjures up so readily. Many of them have been incorporated into this book, so it is entirely fitting and proper that it be dedicated to you, and I do so with love.

Probably the best way to direct my gratitude into the proper channels would be to recognize some of the people who helped me in this project in chronological order, and so I must begin with my publishers, Beverly and Ted Paul of the Beautiful America Publishing Company. When I first mentioned this idea to Ted, he was the first publisher of the several who had expressed an interest to come forth with a contract backed up with hard cash. Since then I have found them to be very compatible folks, knowledgeable in the trade, and willing to work with me in all aspects of my task to make this an artistic as well as a financial success. Also I must commend Ted who knows of my continued interest in good food and wine: every visit with him winds up in some good restaurant with civilized dining and conversation, and he has yet to repeat himself. Now that's class!

Unless you have a good friend of your own, you may find it hard to understand just how much I appreciate the hospitality and friendship of John Wentland and his charming wife, Shirley. His beautiful home in Portland has for several years always had a guest room made up for me, and if ever I spent a night in Portland away from their home, they would feel hurt, and I would feel stupid because no commercial establishment, however fancy, could ever provide the warmth and hospitality this wonderful couple has extended to me. The evenings I have spent with John listening to our mutually appreciated classical music, or the lively discussions in which we easily solved the world's most complicated problems stand out in my mind as some of the most precious moments in our forty-year-old friendship. My sincere thanks to you, John and Shirley, for memories that are pure gold to me.

Another set of old friends whose paths have crossed my own several times is Sam and Dorothy Churchill. I would never think of coming through Astoria without stopping to have a cup of coffee with these two delightful people, and more often than not having lunch with them. They are both knowledgeable in the annals of their historic city, and some of the stories they told me have worked their way into our narrative. My sincere thanks to you both for your help and friendship.

Apparently, Astoria is a friendly town. I also owe a vote of thanks to a very gracious lady who let me trespass on her neaty groomed lawn for some shots of the Astoria-Megler Bridge, and when I thought I had an even better viewpoint, to Mr. Edwin Pye who let me climb to the roof of his house for the shot. I also extend my sincere appreciation to Lt. Michael Monteith, USCG, and to Chief Petty Officer Mike Coe, who really knows how to run a forty-foot cutter through her paces, especially over the Columbia Bar. To all the men and women of the Ilwaco Coast Guard Station, my sincere and heartfelt thanks for a memorable afternoon.

The Olympic Peninsula is justly regarded as one of the wildest spots left in the country, and its penetration sometimes means a few days' abstention from the creature comforts one takes for granted. Maybe that's why my good friends Nat and Barbara Vale pamper me so whenever I stop to visit them at Port Townsend before I plunge into the interior. Actually the glow engendered by the friendship of these two wonderful friends would last for days, but Barbara insists on plying me with her wonderful cooking and Nat with wines from his well-stocked cellar so that every visit becomes a sybaritic experience. Believe me, my gratitude is deep, and will be returned in kind when I can lure them back to my own home in Walla Walla.

While I'm on the Olympic Peninsula I should also tender thanks to Forks Lions Club and especially to Artie Anderson for his help in setting up my coverage of the Fourth of July Celebration the likes of which I have never seen before. Harold Schild, of the Tillamook Farmers' Co-operative, was my guide during a special, behind the scenes tour of his highly interesting plant, and has my thanks. Connie Langley of the Soleduck resort got me into hot water and made me love it when she graciously offered an interesting tour of her spa. The dip was wonderful, and is fondly remembered. Down in the Quinault Ranger District, Ranger Pete Erben showed me where the best views of the rain-forests could be had, and his directions led me to some fascinating country which I will always remember. For that, I am deeply grateful.

To record the wonders of Highway 101, I necessarily traveled the length of the road not once, but several times. That is hardly a hardship when I could indulge my passion for outdoor living. The summer nights I spent outdoors under the stars are some of the most pleasant I have experienced in a lifetime studded with pleasant outdoor experiences. When I got down to more settled areas, the nights I spent in motels are mostly eminently forgettable, with a couple of memorable exceptions. One would hardly class a resort like Salishan as a motel, but I certainly owe a vote of thanks to Pierre Alarco and his staff for making me feel at home in their wonderful

Near Leggett, a section of the original Highway 101 clings precariously to a cliff overlooking the South Fork of the Eel River.

The comparatively gentle curves of the modern Highway 101 near Brookings, in Southern Oregon, offer one breath-taking view after another. The old road was even more scenic, but so frightening that the driver never got to enjoy the scenery.

resort. Another notable exception is the Madonna Inn and its dynamic owner, Alex Madonna. Either one would be memorable, but the combination of the two is absolutely unforgettable. . .and believe me, the experience is gratefully remembered.

Big cities can be very impersonal, but not when you have as gracious a host as Mario Gangitano, who not only showed me the wonders of Orange County, but who provided a very welcome base of operations for my pictorial forays into San Diego and Los Angeles. Mario is a fine Italian chef, and the exotic spaghetti he concocted goes down in my list of gourmet meals I have experienced in a life dedicated on large part to some very fine eating.

While we are on that subject, it would be hard to overlook Rolf Rheinschmitt, a backwoods genius of a chef who was always ready to astound me with something different and wonderful. Passing by Rolf's without stopping would be akin to visiting Rome for a week and never seeing St. Peter's. My sincere thanks to you, Rolf, and know that my gratitude runs very deeply.

My association with the Wine Country of California has always been very pleasant, and not a little of that springs from the fact that it is the home of Joe and Alice Heitz. Their charming little guest house, the "Heitz Hilton" I christened it many years ago, was always open to me, and Joe and Alice, as always, made me feel right at home in the Napa Valley. Joe is a font of information not only on the wine scene, but also on a host of other subjects, and I have liberally tapped this source of information and fine wine, for any meeting with these old friends usually entails the decanting of a few bottles of very noble lineage. As always, Joe and Alice, you are "family" to me, and so no formal thanks are necessary, but you have them anyway.

No visit to the Napa Valley is complete without a tennis match with Margrit Biever, who secretly hopes to some day capture that bottle of Parducci port which I intend to drink on my hundredth birthday. So far, I am ahead, but the visits I have had with Margrit and her husband, Robert Mondavi, are always so pleasant that I am afraid I may some day succumb, and if I ever do, Margrit, be assured that I expect you to keep that bottle till we can drink it together at the proper time. My thanks to you both for visits that are invariably a pleasure and a reflection of the friendship we share along with the wonderful food and wine that are always a complement of those visits. Thanks, thank you very much for some wonderful memories.

The Napa Valley has no monopoly on Wine Country hospitality. My sojourn along 101 made it possible for me to continue a long friendship with John and Margaret Parducci. John is an authority on the wine scene in Mendocino country, and some of the liquid gold he poured for me as a complement to Margaret's exquisite meal in itself would be sufficient reason to do a separate book every year. Believe me, my gratitude is deep.

More thanks are due to Lisa Covington, Public Information Officer for the California Department of Highways who promptly and generously answered a request for information on the building of the Redwood Highway with a wealth of material, some of it an exercise in ingenuity. My thanks also to Mary Hanel, historian for Caltrans who contributed the story of Big Diamond. Help like this makes it possible for a technological achievement to become a much more personal experience, and is very much appreciated. My sincere thanks also go to Lyle Burt, of the Washington Department of Highways, whose help did much to inform me on several aspects of the early days of Highway 101 that would have escaped me otherwise.

When I was trying to get an evening shot of the Golden Gate Bridge, I was hampered by two things: an ignorance of how to get to the best view point, and the absence of a spot where I could park. My thanks to California Highway Patrol Officer Mike Sherman who solved both problems for me. Thanks are also due to officer Gerald Gonzales of the Willits Police Department who gave me the local evaluation of the Skunk trains. I am also grateful to officer Rafael Pata of the San Rafael Police Department who graciously gave up part of his coffee break to pose for me in a carabinieri uniform once worn by his grandfather in Italy. Fortunately, all my associations with the gendarmerie during the making of this book have been a pleasure.

An indispensable part of my equipment during the making of this book, as important to me as my cameras or my notebook was Ole Beulah; my tough, battered old station wagon that without a hitch or a bobble faithfully carried me from one end of 101 to the other at least four times, and over innumerable segments many times more. There was a reason for that unfailing service, and his name is Bruce Gordon. My son-in-law is an engineer, and nowhere was his mechanical expertise more evident than in the impromptu repairs he devised for Ole Beulah, many of which would have baffled the car's original designers. They worked, and when, at the end of the trail Ole Beulah gracefully yielded up her mechanical soul, Bruce still had plans to resurrect her. Looking at her sleek, unscarred successor, I wonder if I'll ever have the heart to take her to some of the places Ole Beulah chewed up in stride. Probably not, she's too pretty. But if ever she needs an ingenious modification, I know who is willing to stay up half the night . . . or more, if need be, to get me back onto the road. My thanks to you, Bruce, not only for the mechanical help, but for the warm and gracious hospitality that makes your home my own.

The most difficult of all my "thank you"'s has been saved for last, because it is not easy to express sentiments that are so deeply felt that mere words somehow become pitifully inadequate. So it is when I try to tell my little Irish wife, my beloved Gadget, how much I appreciate the tender, loving support and understanding she has shown not only during the making of this book, but also over the many years that she has been my best friend as well as the most perfect helpmate any man could ever hope to have. We missed quite a few nights and days together, Gadget, while this book was in the making. I would count these days as missing from my life were it not for the fact that on those lonely nights in the redwoods, my mind would dwell lovingly on the times when you and I explored this wonderland together, and as always, in spirit you were there beside me, as you forever are in my heart.

Earl Roberge
Walla Walla, Wa.

Near Destruction Island, on Washington's Olympic Coast, a summer sunset adds to a beauty that is already overwhelming.

The Avenue of the Giants, near Redcrest, California, is the old Highway 101, and winds through thirty miles of the most inspiring redwood groves in existence.

FOREWORD

During the time Earl Roberge was in the Napa Valley working on his NAPA WINE COUNTRY book, I came to appreciate his talent and dedication. In his photos and text, he captured the elusive magic of the Napa Valley, and made it come alive for all to see. These were the comparatively early days of the Valley, in which we also played a part, and we feel that Earl's description of the Valley had much to do with its present fame.

Earl met with the vintners, their families, their staffs, and portrayed the life in the vineyards and the cellars. With his able brush he painted a lively and romantic picture, getting the essence of each winery and its people. Sometimes he subtly caught an evocative moment with a light, deft touch; at others a feeling or event was painted with bold strokes. His language was usually simple and straightforward, but often, swayed by the beauty of the valley he learned to love, became downright poetic.

It is nice to see that he has not lost his touch. Now, under his able guidance, we visit the most beautiful landmarks of one of the world's most interesting highways, the world famous U.S. 101. Earl has traveled and researched this long road from the Mexican border to within sight of Canada's Vancouver Island, with meticulous interest and with his introspective eye, always catching the best angle for a picture, or the most revealing story to be found along the way. He even shares his intimate knowledge of the highway, whether it be a restaurant with civilized fare or a hidden beauty spot not usually found by the average traveler. With his keen eye for beauty, he teaches us to see, not merely look, and thus makes the journey along U.S. 101 a delight.

I saw him discover the Napa Valley for what it really is, but adding additional luster to an already sparkling gem with his own personal touch. So it is with his book on U.S. 101: his photographs and text make every vignette come alive in an exciting way, making you turn each page with great anticipation, and when, regretfully, you reach the end, you feel you have really shared a great adventure that has enriched your life. There can be no better reason for a great book.

Robert Mondavi

Robert Mondavi, at home on Wappo Hill.

Napa Valley, home of some of the world's finest wines, as seen from the Spring Mountain Road.

INTRODUCTION

It begins at the Tijuana-San Ysidro border crossing and heads toward Los Angeles as a crowded freeway. At the Orange County line it is finally marked U.S. 101 and continues northward through Oregon and Washington for a total of 1644.4 miles. At its most northerly point, the peaks of Canada's Vancouver Island soar above the Straits of Georgia, and at night the lights outlining the Parliament buildings in Victoria cast a ruddy glow into the darkened sky.

This is Highway 101, the direct descendant of the old Spanish El Camino Real, and one of the most varied, fascinating, and picturesque highways ever created by man. Embellished by Nature with vistas of great cities, seacoasts, and varied forests, it possesses a rare beauty that makes it unique amongst the highways of the world.

Diversity is the hallmark of this highway. In its southernmost stretches it passes through a region that would be a desert were it not for the miracle of irrigation, and in its northernmost parts it penetrates a jungle-like rain-forest tropical in its luxuriance. For the greater part of its length it is within the sight, sound, smell or climatic influence of the Pacific Ocean, and the stunning vistas it offers of the edge of a continent are a large part of its fascination. It is at times an eight-lane freeway choked with wall-to-wall traffic, and at others a narrow country road tunnelling through seemingly interminable walls of verdure. Sometimes it winds through crowded cities like a well-fed anaconda, and at others threads its way past isolated hamlets where service stations are thirty miles or more apart. In the redwood country it shoulders its way through stands of majestic trees soaring like an arboreal cathedral, two hundred feet to the first limb, and on the Olympic Peninsula skirts the wildest coast in the contiguous United States. Along the California and Oregon coasts, it often clings precariously to a narrow shelf blasted out of the edge of the continent with the roar and crash of an angry surf surging at its base, seemingly ready to wash it into the ocean. It is a road of inspiring beauty and of utter desolation; of frenetic activity and quiet solitude: sometimes it is as straight as well-stretched string, and at others, its curves limit visibility to fifty feet . . .or less. There may be a few of its 1644.4 miles that could be considered dull, but these fade into insignificance compared to the many hundreds of miles affording some of the most enchanting vistas to be found on this planet.

A great highway is more than merely a means of getting from Point A to Point B. It is the thread on which the events of a whole region are strung: the vital, throbbing artery through which the life of a region pulses, and if it serves its utilitarian purpose with the added fillip of beauty, then it becomes more of an adventure than merely a road.

Highway 101 does this with a consummate ease, and for this reason, it is a worthy subject for this book.

Anyone faced with the plethora of material a subject of this kind offers faces a difficult choice. How do you approach such a large and varied subject? Do you make it a definitive book, listing everything pertinent to it? Not practical! The book would be a tome a foot thick, and in its profusion of material more like a government report, and about as interesting. Do you take only the spectacular parts of the highway? Again, not practical: 101 is spectacular for a large part of its total length, and besides, some of the more interesting things along its route may not be classed as spectacular. You'd wind up with another fifty-pound book. Do you dwell on the history that has taken place along this route? That in itself is material for several books, and while it is an intriguing subject that necessarily will be approached, it is not the whole story. How, then, do you tell the story of a road that is not only an adventure in beauty, but also a look at the whole lifestyle of a varied and fascinating region?

As is usually the case, the answer is so simple that it could easily be overlooked: don't try to eat the whole, enormous pie, no matter how tempting it may be; take just a few tasty pieces, as your hunger dictates, and tasting thoroughly, enjoy them at your leisure. You certainly will not get to eat the whole pie, but neither will you experience the intellectual indigestion that would have been yours had you tried, and this way you will have pleasant memories of the feast, and a reservoir of future adventures.

This is what I suggest we do: I will take you on a vicarious trip the length of Highway 101, starting at the Mexican Border. We do not have to stay strictly on the highway: there are fascinating side trips a few miles off the main route, and some of these we will explore, but generally we will stay on the main road as it traverses the length of California, Oregon, and Washington from south to north.

A few miles north of Crescent City, we become guests of the state of Oregon, and travel the full length of that beautiful state along the world-famous Oregon Coast. At Astoria, we cross the soaring Astoria-Megler Bridge and enter the Evergreen State, Washington. 101 follows the edge of the Olympic Peninsula, past recently-logged sites of horrible ugliness, and then, as though embarrassed by this momentary lapse from its customary beauty, past an aquamarine lake astounding in its perfection. With Canada in sight across the Straits of Georgia, the road dips to the south along the magic vistas of Hood Canal, and finally merges with Interstate 5 at Olympia in the shadow of the capitol dome. Quite a trip, and one that, once made, will never be forgotten. I have made it several times, and each time I have found new sights, new experiences, new adventures. One thing it never has been is dull, maybe because I am the first to admit that I have not yet seen anywhere near all that the highway has to offer, and every trip brings some new revelation.

One thing should be realized and accepted, even though reluctantly: it simply is not possible, in one or even several lifetimes, to absorb all that the highway has to offer. Even a long-lived traveler would miss something, and while this may sometimes be frustrating, it also holds out a promise of future discoveries every time the trip is made. Columbus discovered a New World, but, almost five centuries later, the New World he found has not yet been completely explored, and every day yields up a few more of its many fascinating secrets.

So it will be with 101. We will discover a whole new world, and while this trip we will make together may be called a first voyage of discovery, I must leave it up to each individual traveler to make his or her subsequent explorations. If I can implant in my fellow travelers the desire to look, and not merely see, to listen, and not merely hear, then your lives will be enriched by the experience of traveling this great highway, as mine has been. I will try to share with you some of the things I have found along 101, secure in the knowledge that the things I have found interesting are of a sufficiently generic nature that they will also be interesting to the great majority of our readers.

So, let's make a beginning.

At the Tijuana-San Ysidro border crossing, an enterprising Mexican street vendor displays his wares so that anyone who was too busy in Tijuana to absorb the local culture can prove that he was really there.

CHAPTER REFERENCE MAP

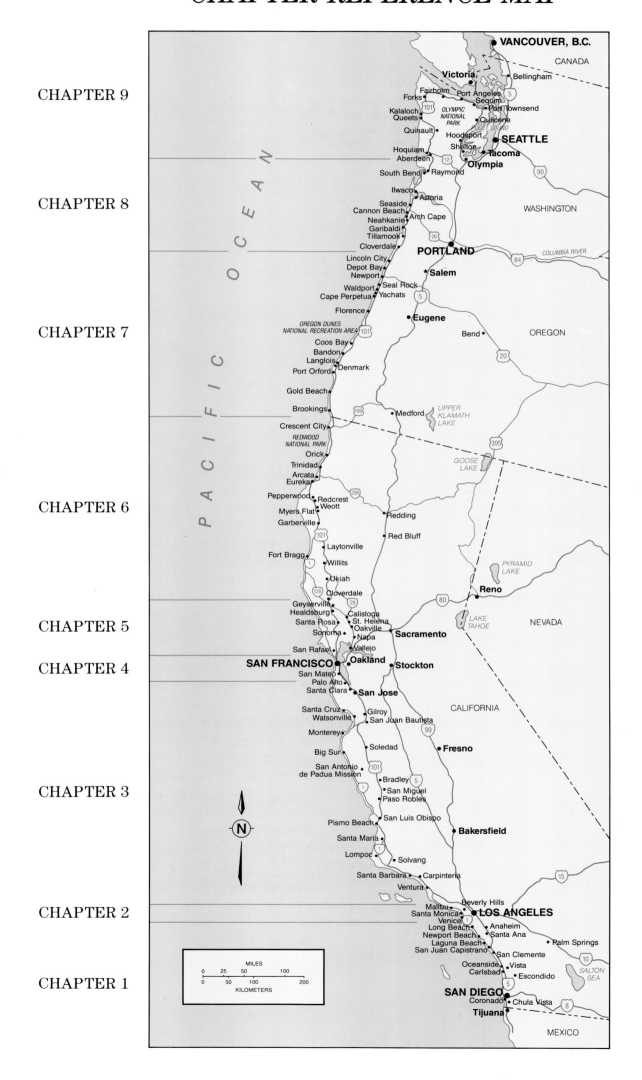

CHAPTER 1

EL CAMINO REAL

It will come as somewhat of a surprise to most Americans that Southern California, comprising as it does some of the choicest and most valuable real estate in the world was virtually ignored by its Spanish owners for over two centuries. While considerable time, effort, and treasure was expended developing the wastelands of Baja California (Lower California) the beautiful and fertile lands of Alta California (Upper California) remained empty of white occupancy until the latter part of the eighteenth century.

Charles III of Spain saw in the wars in which France and Great Britain were embroiled in the middle of the eighteenth century a chance to burnish the luster of the badly tarnished Spanish crown. Spain's explorers had for two centuries ranged the Pacific Coast as far north as Vancouver Island, as a host of Spanish place-names will testify, so they were no strangers to these parts. The development of the new lands, however, went to Baja California, which was better situated to trans-ship overland to Mexico the treasures brought by the plate fleets from the rich Peruvian mines, and to service the galleons trading with the Spanish outposts in the Philippines. Alta California was known, jealously possessed, but uninhabited by white men.

An enlightened and energetic monarch, Charles III was determined to exploit the discoveries of Sebastian Viscaino and especially of Juan Cabrillo, who, in 1542 had discovered a magnificent bay in Alta California. An expedition headed by Gaspar de Portola was dispatched by sea, and at the same time orders were given to an obscure Franciscan friar stationed in Baja California to join the expedition by land.

On July 16, 1769, Portola raised the standard of Spain, fired a cannon, and founded a presidio on the shores of that bay—the first white settlement in present-day California. On the same day, the foot-sore Franciscan friar raised a cross, rang a bell, and founded the mission of San Diego de Alcala. The echoes of that mission bell were destined to ring down the pages of history long after the cannon-shot had become a mere historical footnote.

The movement that Fra Junipéro Serra initiated that day was destined to shape the future of California, for the mission he founded at San Diego was the first in a chain that eventually reached as far north as Sonoma. That this indomitable Franciscan, sick, tired, already an old man, was able to conquer one of the world's most formidable obstacle courses, Baja California, and still be able to start an oasis of civilization in the southern desert is a story in itself, and one we shall visit in a subsequent chapter. Kind and gentle by nature but burning with a zeal that could transform him into a veritable lion on occasion, this remarkable man founded eight more missions before his wasted body was laid to rest beneath the flagstone of his beloved Mission Carmel. The part he plays in our story is that each of those missions was a day's journey apart; about thirty miles, and the trail connecting them soon grew into a road: El Camino Real, the Royal Road, the direct ancestor of present-day 101.

In our journey along the Southern Californian

part of Highway 101, we will be retracing the steps of those gray-clad Franciscans. Yes, gray-clad, for the brown habit worn by today's Franciscans was not adopted till 1890. Really, the color of the habits was immaterial, for in a half-hour's trip along El Camino Real everything, clothes, hair, faces was soon covered with a thick layer of gray dust raised by the hooves of the slowly plodding burros. While we will be following the some route, we will be doing it in considerable more comfort and with a daily rate of progress that would have a raised a shade of envy even in the saintly soul of Fra Junipéro Serra.

Still, let's not go too quickly: the plan was to take small bites out of the whole pie and to savor those bites to the full. Therefore, we'll be making a few stops along the way, and take time to smell the flowers.

The obvious place to start a trip is at the beginning; in this case the Mexican border. Anyone going that close to Mexico will want to visit Tijuana, and indeed it is a most interesting city, but our trip is along 101, not amazing the citizens of Tijuana with our version of Castillian Spanish. While getting into Mexico is simply a matter of driving across the border, getting back into the United States is somewhat slower.

There are long lines before each entry lane at the border. An American with the proper documentation and who does not fit the profile of a terrorist or a drug-smuggler can usually get across the border with a minimum of hassle, but if for any reason at all the suspicions of the inspector are aroused, you can expect a rigorous search and an indefinite postponement of our trip together if any contraband is found.

Once you're across the border the signs will read "Interstate 5" and you breath a sigh of relief: you're back in the land of milk and honey and expensive gas. In spite of the freeway signs, you're also on the old El Camino Real, masquerading as Interstate 5 to the Orange County Line, where the highway is once more correctly marked.

Our first sight of the city that Gaspar de Portola founded is apt to be the soaring concrete arch of the bridge joining San Diego to Coronado on the opposite side of the bay. The view from the Coronado side is worth the dollar bridge toll, and the return trip is free. There is a nice little park at the first exit after the bridge and the view of the San Diego skyline, especially at sunset when all the skyscrapers are painted a tawny gold by the setting sun is absolutely magnificent.

San Diego is a very pleasant city with probably the best over-all climate in the whole country. The adjacent ocean keeps the city from getting too warm in the summer, or too cold in the winter, so that flowers grow the year round, and springtime lasts for ten months of the year. Not surprisingly, the population of San Diego has grown by leaps and bounds, especially since thousands of Navy personnel, having taken their first tasty sip of the climate during their tour of duty here, decide that life is too short to continually fight snow and slush, and make this their permanent home. The Eleventh Naval District makes San Diego its base, with the result that a good part of the Pacific Fleet is stationed here, and a trip along the waterfront will usually reward us with the sight of a few battle-gray cruisers or aircraft carriers home for repairs or shore leave.

As we might expect from the second largest city in California, San Diego offers all kinds of diversions. Since our trip does not usually entail a prolonged stay in any one area, we'll have to skim the cream, so to speak, and take in some of the more obvious highlights. Naturally, we'll have to see the San Diego Zoo, whose imaginative and innovative ways of showing off its exotic animals have made it one of the outstanding zoos of the world. Adjacent Balboa Park is also well-worth a visit, as an example of what tropical verdure can achieve in a desert clime if given sufficient water. Wear comfortable walking shoes, be prepared to walk a few miles and bring your camera: photo opportunities abound.

Another place where your camera absolutely must go is Sea World, a few miles north of the city center. In a large open-air aquarium, killer whales and superbly trained porpoises put on a stunning show of acrobatics, which, for the volume of water displaced is unequaled anywhere in the world. The highly intelligent aquatic animals seem to actually enjoy putting on a display of aerial acrobatics that would make a trained gymnast green with envy, and often come up with unrehearsed but highly entertaining—and perfectly synchronized—leaps and re-entries that leave the spectators breathless, and also sometimes thoroughly soaked. Sea World is the home of the first killer whale born in captivity, and the new-born calf is rapidly becoming a star in his own right. I'd love to show you pictures of this wonderful show, but as much as the management will encour-

(Overleaf) Alioso Beach, near Laguna Beach, offers a rocky break in the smooth stretch of sand that has made the Southern California beaches so famous.

age you to take pictures for your personal enjoyment, they absolutely refuse to allow any of them to be used commercially...and that includes pictures used in a book. Anyway, I tried!

People enchanted with the aura of perpetual Spring that permeates the whole San Diego area will probably find the best expression of that condition in La Jolla, a suburb of San Diego a few miles north of the city center. Although it is part of the municipality of San Diego, it has a mystique all of its own that somehow sets it apart. Picturesquely perched on cliffs overlooking the Pacific, it is a place of flowers, sea-birds, superb vistas and good restaurants where the year-round attire leans strongly to tennis togs. Quite obviously a haven of the affluent, it also is home to Scripps Aquarium, part of the School of Oceanography, University of California, San Diego Branch. The aquarium and tide pools are beautifully maintained and stocked and are a deservedly popular tourist attraction. Large collections of fish, some of them of really formidable size, live in tenuous harmony, and apparently have become accustomed to the idea that humans find them extremely interesting as well as edible. Definitely worth the small detour off Interstate 5 that the stop entails.

The trip northward from San Diego to the Orange County Line is, frankly, not one of the beautiful stretches of El Camino Real. The land is mostly flat, sagebrush-covered desert, and would be an unbroken monotony were it not for the almost continuous home and office development fronting on the freeway. Actually, this is land that only a real estate developer with a large, skilled, and extremely motivated staff could love, but the fact that the land adjacent to the freeway is at a premium apparently testifies that the lure of living in the land of the eternal Spring is a very potent one. The monotony of the trip is broken by a nuclear plant near San Clemente, and the desert terrain of the Marine Corps base of Camp Pendleton, crisscrossed by the trails of armored personnel carriers which have left scars on the fragile desert ecology which are very nearly permanent.

Many of our marines are trained here, and if the county in which they are trained is any indication of their fighting effectiveness, they are indeed as tough fighting-men as the legends make them out to be.

In spite of the desert locale, there are several towns along the route, San Clemente being a good example. This is the land of the surfer and the best-stuffed bikinis this side of Ipanima: mile after mile of flat, sandy beaches, continually leveled by huge combers, and the haunt of eager young surfers obsessed with a never-ending search for the perfect wave.

A very popular sport world-wide, but one which here has been raised to the level of a fine art, is "bird watching." In this case, the "birds" are the legendary blonde, bronzed, long-legged golden girls of California. Clad, in a fashion, in minuscule bikinis, and epitomizing in their freedom all the glamor of this part of the world, they add a highly decorative touch to an otherwise drab stretch of ocean beach. Their male counterparts, the equally blonde and bronzed beach-boys, are apt to be up at dawn, getting in a few hours of their favorite sport before they cursingly depart for the more mundane task of making a living. In truth, the parade of so much bronzed flesh is so ubiquitous that it is taken very much for granted by the beach devotees, many of whom are ogling each other as much as they are the opposite sex. For these people, the worst, most implacable and fiercely fought enemy, is Father Time, for this is the land of the youth cult; and almost anyone reaching the age of thirty feels that life, of at least that part of it which is meaningful, has ended.

A glance at the map will tell us that San Juan Capistrano and its famous mission are just ahead. Let's stop and take a look, but since we will have a whole chapter later on devoted to the missions, let's make this a short visit and come back here later when we can linger awhile. Probably the best known of all the missions because of its famous punctual swallows, it is mostly in ruins, but the ruins are impressive enough to bring thousands of visitors each year to another one of Fra Serra's missions.

San Juan Capistrano is also a good place to temporarily forsake the freeway for a parallel route, U.S. 1 which follows the beach more closely and is a welcome relief from the wholesale development that fringes El Camino Real all the way to Los Angeles. Not that U.S. 1 does not have its share of development: but the real estate boys haven't yet figured out how to sell the ocean, so at least one side of the road is reasonably the way it was back in the days of the padres.

U.S. 1 is never more than a few miles from the

freeway, but it hugs the beach and runs through a succession of small towns: Capistrano Beach, Laguna Beach, Corona del Mar, Balboa, and finally Newport Beach. Some of the beaches are very picturesque, with rocky headlands interrupting the smooth stretches of sand we found farther south, and most of them are at the door of homes whose owners obviously consider the expense of building in these parts only a minor inconvenience. Laguna Beach is famous as a haven of many contemporary artists, and Newport Beach is Beverly Hills with a sea view.

Newport Beach Center is the place where good shoppers go when they die and go to Heaven. A handsome group of high-rise stores, offices and apartments crowning a rise above the beach, it holds within its confines all the cultural amenities of a small city, as well as unlimited shopping in branches of America's most prestigious stores. Newport Beach itself is definitely not for the average citizen: most of the homes facing the ocean are in the million-dollar-plus class, and many of them several times that. Still, by following the beach road the average person can admire the homes, and I have found some of the people there to be as nice and hospitable as any along the whole length of 101. Wealthy does not necessarily mean snobbish!

Getting back on Interstate 5 is not too difficult: just follow almost any main east-west road, and in time it will intersect with the freeway, which runs north and south. If you see a sign reading "Anaheim," take it, for it will almost surely lead you to that Mecca of the average tourist, Disneyland.

Like Sea World, Disneyland is another place that does not allow commercial use of photographs taken on its premises. Even the architecture is copyrighted and may not be photographed and used without permission from the front office—a bureaucratic jungle that would take days to penetrate. So, we will take a brief un-illustrated peek at this fascinating wonder-world and leave it up to the individual traveler to make his or her own pilgrimage to this land of fantasy.

The freeway exits leading to Disneyland are clearly marked, and parking is readily available. . .at a price, of course. Disneyland is already well-enough known that further description of it would be adding water to an already overflowing bucket, so we will not elaborate on what is probably the world's best known amusement park. Suffice it to say that it is a superb blend of technology with showmanship and fantasy, and the fact that people from all over the world come to this entertainment adventure is sufficient testimony to its excellence. If you want a real iron-clad endorsement, ask a child (of any age) who has been there for an opinion, and watch the eyes gleam as he or she tells you about a never-to-be forgotten visit to a magic kingdom.

Once you have reached Interstate 5, you are in the heart of Orange County, one of the wealthiest counties in the United States, and a paramount purveyor of the good life, Southern California style. The freeway threads right through the county, and while you may look for a long time for one of the orange groves which originally gave the county its name, you will see plenty of the houses and commercial enterprises which have supplanted them. Not from the freeway, however: you'll be too busy fighting the murderous traffic on the Santa Ana Freeway, as this section of the Intestate is called. Anyone desiring to see the residential sections has only to take an exit. . .any one will do, and drive. This is life in the fast lane; the habitat of the overachiever, the wheeler-dealer, where one can make a fortune in a few months and lose it in a few minutes. It is also a place that two million or so almost ordinary, hard-working people gladly call home and would not exchange its smog-laden air and monumental traffic jams for any other place on Earth.

What makes it so wonderful? Just get up at seven a.m. on a winter morning and savor the glory of a Spring-like day in the middle of winter, and you'll have the answer to why so many people are willing to put up with the inconveniences as long as they can also have the benefits. That is one reason, and a very compelling one. Another is that this is the headquarters of many high-tech industries: computers, electronics, aero-space, and that the research centers of the areas are on the cutting edge of the technology that shapes the future. This is a place where a person with ability and the willingness to use it can soar to unequaled heights, and be rewarded accordingly.

It is not Utopia, by any manner or means: the drug problem that plagues the whole country is endemic here, and some minorities experience a sometimes overt and at other times blatant discrimination which hinders them from achieving their full potential. Still, there are social and economic advantages that make the inconveniences pale into,

Coronado Bridge, a soaring steel and concrete arch, connects Coronado to downtown
San Diego.

The skyline of downtown San Diego, deservedly the fastest growing large city
in California.

Near Laguna Beach, flowering ice plants add a touch of color.

The ocean front is largely preempted by luxurious developments, many of which use water in imaginative ways. The entrance to this one is near Laguna Beach.

if not insignificance, at least second place, and millions of people happily call this home.

Interstate 5 to the Los Angeles County border is only one of a maze of freeways all funneling millions of cars into the metropolitan hub of Los Angeles. During the rush traffic hours, it seems as though all the cars in Southern California are trying to do that at the same time; a supposition that is really not far off in fact. The Los Angeles area alone has more cars than most European countries, and a good many of them are headed along El Camino Real toward that magnet of Southern California, Los Angeles.

CHAPTER
2

CITY OF THE ANGELS

With no noticeable change other than in highway signs, we cross from Orange County into the county and city of Los Angeles. The highway is as crowded as ever, but El Camino Real is now officially U.S. 101, and to fit it into the freeway system that sprawls all over Los Angeles County like an octupus having a seizure, it is also called the Hollywood Freeway. To the left, the towers of the central city soar into the smog, and in a short time we pass the site where, on September 1, 1781, the pueblo of La Nuestra Senora, La Reina de Los Angeles began as a municipal entity.

Actually, that peripatetic founder of cities, Gaspar de Portola and his chaplain, Fra Juan Crespi had visited the site on August 2, 1769, and the priest had noted in his journal: "This pleasant site on the Porciuncula River has all the requisites for a large settlement."

He was a good judge of town sites. Los Angeles today is by any standard a very large settlement indeed, with over three million inhabitants within the city proper, and eight million or more in the complex of cities that makes up Los Angeles County. In the last decade, it finally displaced Chicago as the nation's second most populated city, and if it keeps growing at its same rate, may very well be the largest during the lifetime of most of its present inhabitants. In area, its 465 square miles make it the second largest city in the United States, being exceeded only by a small Alaskan village I once visited that had expanded its city limits over a vast area mainly so that, under the state's local option law, it could prohibit liquor from the immediate surroundings.

Los Angeles probably has more inhabitants in just one of its crowded city blocks.

Mere statistics alone somehow are woefully deficient when it comes to describing this sprawling giant. We know that it is big, that it is the chief exponent of a life-style which, to put it kindly, is considered eccentric by the rest of the country, its freeways are legendry, and everyone knows that without the automobile, Los Angeles would cease to exist and self-destruct into a host of smaller cities having only the common characteristics of contiguity. To really get the sight, smell, and feel of this dynamic city, we must visit its stately boulevards, its affluent suburbs, its parks and museums, and even the ghettos that can justly only be described as noisome, because each is part of that fascinating metropolis we call Los Angeles.

Unlike most cities that have long had a clearly delineated central area, Los Angeles is an urban giant that only recently has begun to develop a recognizable center. Following the disastrous 1906 earthquake which decimated San Francisco and badly rattled Los Angeles, city ordinances were passed limiting the height of any building to thirteen stories. These ordinances were conveniently ignored for the building of City Hall in 1928, which at twenty eight stories was for many years the tallest structure within city limits. City Hall still is a very impressive building, but is now dwarfed by a host of skyscrapers which, following the rescission of the thirteen story rule in 1957, sprouted like mushrooms in the previously unimpressive downtown area, and began to give Los Angeles an urban image commensurate

At San Clemente, towering breakers lure surfers to a never-ending search for the perfect wave.

At Laguna Beach, sunbathers are ubiquitous on the warm sandy beach, each one in search of the perfect tan.

with its size.

The problem is that the repeal of the rule also made it possible for skyscrapers to be built in other sections of the city, and they sprouted up piecemeal in no concentrated area, so that the impact of the burgeoning city-center near Old Town was considerably diluted.

This is very possibly a reflection of the outstanding characteristic of the Angelenos: they are the most individualistic characters in the country. Do your own thing: do as you please, whether or not it conforms to the ordinary standards held by the more staid citizens in other parts of the country. As a result, Los Angeles has long held the reputation of having far more than its share of weird characters whose style in clothes, manners, and morals would hardly be accepted in Dubuque. It also has more than its share of leaders and creative people who, by reason of their dominant position in the communications arts, have helped to in time make their ways the accepted norm all over the country. Three-quarters of all the movies on the United States are still planned or completely made in Hollywood and nearby Burbank, and the stream of TV programs emanating from their studios have much to do with shaping the life-style and morals of a nation which, consciously or unconsciously, shapes its own life on the pattern set by the entertainment media. It has been truly said that California is the trend-setter in the United States, and it is equally true that Los Angeles sets the trend in California.

This is all background for our small foray into Los Angeles, for since 101 cuts through it, it is definitely part of our exploration of this highway, and a decidedly interesting detour. Before we can intelligently tackle the city, a few basic principles should be mastered. The first of these is a good map of the city and county, and the second is the ability to use that map, especially to master the freeway system. Also, we should thoroughly condition ourselves to the idea that in Los Angeles all the usual activities and necessities of life: food, transportation, employment, even entertainment, are all related to the automobile. In all other parts of the country, a person without access to a car is a rarity: in Los Angeles, such a person would be a non-entity.

The freeways of Los Angeles have a fearsome reputation, not all of which is well-deserved. Personally, I enjoy driving in Los Angeles because everyone there knows the freeway rules and, if only for self-survival, more or less obeys them. There are not many bad drivers left in Los Angeles: most of them have been killed off years ago and the survivors have necessarily adapted to conditions that would panic anyone except a Roman chariot driver. One of the first things we'll have to learn is patience. If the freeway is clogged because of an accident, we may as well resign ourselves to crawling along, bumper to bumper, until the jam is cleared because we have no real alternative. Tempers as well as cooling systems may sometimes boil, and lately the freeways have regretably become shooting galleries as frustrated drivers sometimes vent their anger with automatic weapons. Still, it is the best available way of getting from point A to point B, and with a little advance planning not an impossible task.

Before we start exploring Los Angeles, maybe we should sort out its various components. "Los Angeles" can mean either the area within city limits, which sprawls all over the place, from the San Fernando Valley to the sea at San Pedro, the municipal area, which is even larger and is made up of cities contiguous but not politically part of Los Angeles, and the county, which is as large as half the state of Vermont and has a population larger than all but eight states. A lot of artful gerrymandering went on in early days, mostly to keep desirable sections within city limits. For example, the port area, down by San Pedro, is connected to the city by a narrow corridor twenty-five miles long, flanked on both sides by municipalities which are in Los Angeles County, but not strictly speaking part of the city of Los Angeles. We'll have a hard time telling, when we cross from one to the other, when the change occurs: it's all megalopolis, and we're still in Greater Los Angeles.

This political subdivision has an interesting background. Before the urban sprawl that made Los Angeles one continuous city in fact, if not politically, there were several small towns and villages which were completely separate from Los Angeles, and actually isolated from each other. When the water of the Owens Valley was brought to a thirsty Los Angeles in 1913, any community that wanted to partake of this very welcome bonanza had to become part of the city. Some communities, Beverly Hills and Hollywood, for example, declined to do so, and instead bought their water, which considerably enriched those entrepreneurs who had brought the water to the area largely using municipal funds. So

Los Angeles' freeways are justly famous, and this interchange at Antelope Junction on Interstate 5 is an example of how those intertwining roads are finally unscrambled. There are five levels of freeways here, and at times each one of them is simultaneously exhibiting bumper to bumper traffic.

As well known as the freeways, the famed Los Angeles smog spreads its pall over the city. This view of the city center is from the tower of the Los Angeles County Court House, and the smog this day was not particularly bothersome. However, it certainly negated the long-range photo we had planned, to show you how vast this sprawling city really is.

it is that to this day Beverly Hills is a separate town, not subject to Los Angeles ordinances, with its own city government, police and fire departments, yet it is completely surrounded by the city of Los Angeles and is indubitably a part of the metropolitan complex.

Another town known the world over, Hollywood, was founded in 1887 by Horace Wilcox, a strict Prohibitionist who laid out what was intended to be a sober, highly moral, God-fearing community. The almost year-round sunshine with which it is favored and its proximity to a variety of locales made it an early choice for the motion picture industry, then very much dependent on natural sunlight, and little by little a transformation began that must have Horace whirling in his grave like a pinwheel. Hollywood and nearby Burbank still account for a large part of the motion pictures produced in the United States, even though more and more productions are being moved to other locales that have lower production costs. Still, when the ultimate in quality is desired, the productions are apt to be locally made, because no other area has better facilities or a larger pool of talent.

It is paradoxical that Sunset Boulevard, which runs through Hollywood and for many years epitomized the glamor that was synonymous whith that name, has a mile-long section known locally as "The Strip" which has become notorious as a drug-ridden haven for young addicts and prostitutes, both male and female, who make it their hang-out. Many a small-town beauty queen bedazzled by the adulation her comeliness has brought her in her small Midwest or Southern town arrives in town with stars in her eyes, intent on having the city at her feet. The harsh realities of life in the big city come crashing down on her in short order. Beauty, in Hollywood, is a common commodity, for this exodus to the movie capitol has been going on for three generations, and many of the beauty queens of yesteryear who never made it into the movies became enamored of the city and stayed, breeding good-looking children who form a ready pool of home-grown talent.

The latest arrivals usually stay until their money runs out and then if they are sufficiently intelligent, go back home and marry that nice young dentist or teacher. The more stupid ones stay and stubbornly keep trying. A few, a very few, make it into the industry, but by far the greater majority become waitresses, or if they aren't that lucky, usually the teen-aged prostitutes that throng "The Strip" . . . now a veritable Boulevard of Broken Dreams.

Armed with our map and a general plan of what we'd like to see, let's tackle Los Angeles. One of the most interesting sites in the city is the La Brea Tar Pits, just off Wilshire Boulevard. Here, in prehistoric times, an area of asphalt based oil-seeps had for centuries been trapping the cave bears, saber-tooth tigers, and giant sloths that infested the area, and the asphalt had preserved their bones perfectly. It is fortunate for us that these pits are conveniently located on Wilshire Boulevard, one of the most spacious and easily negotiated main streets of Los Angeles. Starting from the downtown area, we proceed northward to our first stop, MacArthur Park.

The park, unfortunately, is overrun with people, drug-pushers, and geese that have never been house-broken. There is some grass left, but in the most popular area, down by the duck pond, large sections of the park have been worn down to bare, hard-packed dirt: a classic case of over-use. This is the haunt of the small-time drug peddler, at least one of whom had his stash of marijuana hidden under one of the park trash-barrels. After a furtive look-around to make sure no policeman is watching, the drum is quickly tipped, a few reefers or glassine envelopes of cocaine are quickly passed on to the customer and exchanged for cash. Sad, that in this spot that could be so beautiful with its pond and view of beautiful high-rises, human depravity is common.

The 5800 block of Wilshire Boulevard fronts on the La Brea Tar Pits, where a self-guided tour will lead us to the excavations that have uncovered skeletons of the animals that had wandered into the sticky tar-seeps that to this day ooze out of the ground from the depths of the subterranean oil fields. Stay on the paths: we are on top of an oil-field, and indeed quite a few of the surrounding buildings camouflage oil-pumping operations which, on aesthetic grounds, have been hidden from public view. They present no danger, but the seeps can be pretty messy, and the way it sticks to our clothes will show us why the early settlers made liberal use of this material as a waterproofing agent. The George C. Page Museum of La Brea Discoveries adjacent to the pits has reconstructed skeltons of mammoths and mastodons and is well worth a visit.

We might as well continue along Wilshire Boulevard: it is a pleasant drive and it goes directly through Beverly Hills, an affluent enclave of the very rich which has its own distinct personality. Here is Rodeo Drive, famous as the haunt of those to whom money has no real meaning, and the famous ultra-polite police who, if we park our car on almost any street will appear in minutes and ask how they can help us out. Unless we have a pretty convincing reason for being there, the "out" will be out of Beverly Hills. The homes are fabulous, but not many of them are visible from the street: high walls with electronic gates and elaborate security systems guarantee that the sybaritic life-style which has become synonymous with Beverly Hills will be enjoyed in privacy.

If we stay on Wilshire Boulevard long enough, it will eventually lead us to Santa Monica, where we are faced with a choice. Go right, along Pacific Highway, which is U.S. 1, and we'll go past Pacific Palisades and Malibu, and eventually join 101 at Ventura. Since this would take us out of Los Angeles and we still have quite a few more things to see, let's turn left and go along U.S. 1 toward Santa Monica, Venice, and eventually, Long Beach.

Santa Monica and Venice both are famous for their beaches, and they're great . . . if we can find a place to park. On a warm summer afternoon when a million or so Angelenos converge on the beaches to take part in the carnival that is taking place there, that is something of an accomplishment. If, however, we can get anywhere near the ocean we can become part of the famous California beach scene. Here is the northern extension of the southern beaches we have already seen, complete with volleyball games, beach parties, and acres of reddening flesh, most of it considerably more exposed than the law allows. Here also is the famous "Muscle Beach" where body builders congregate to display their over-sized deltoids and strike up relationships notorious for their variety and brevity. It's an atmosphere of hot dogs, hamburgers and funny cigarette smoke, but it's something we must see if we want to say that we've seen Los Angeles.

The road south goes through beach communities merging the one with the other with no discernible break. We make a detour around Marina Del Rey, billed as the world's largest pleasure boat port, and if we happen to be here late in the afternoon, watch a seemingly endless string of pleasure boats cruising back to their berths along the man-made harbor. A quick mental calculation of all the disposable income this represents runs into the millions so quickly that we give up in a few minutes.

Another port, but much larger, is at San Pedro, Los Angeles' deep water port and the site of Port O' Cal Village, a pleasant collection of restaurants, gift shops and bars, all designed to separate the visiting tourist from his petty, or not so petty, cash. Well worth the time it takes to visit, especially if we have a few hours to dawdle away, and that intriguing young salt with the concertina and a vast collection of salty sea-chanties is still in residence. Taking in all the wonders displayed here for our amazement would take hours, and if we stay long enough, we may see a familiar-looking white cruise-ship setting out to sea. This is the *Sea Princess* of "Love Boat" fame, and San Pedro is her base on the Pacific Coast. Don't expect to see all handsome, unattached young men and nubile young women crowding her rails: the passenger list runs more to properly married middle-aged and retired couples taking that once-in-a-lifetime cruise, although the publicity engendered by the popular TV series has certainly increased the number of young people aboard, all intent on perpetuating the antics for which the Love Boat has become famous, or infamous, depending on your point of view.

We're almost in Long Beach now, and two things here, both large and world-famous, we must not miss. One is the *Spruce Goose*, longer than a football field, eight stories high, and still the world's largest airplane. It is hangared in a vast geodesic dome after its only flight of a few miles, which was done primarily to prove to Howard Hughes that his monstrous eight-engined creation could really fly. Also of more than passing interest to a generation of young people by-passed by the glamorous era of trans-Atlantic ship travel is the *Queen Mary*, permanently berthed here, dwarfing her surroundings with her imposing height, and giving the tourists some idea of just how luxurious ship-board life could be before the more utilitarian jumbo jet took over the task of mass transportation to Europe. A self-guided tour lets us visit both attractions at our leisure.

We're south of Los Angeles now, and maybe we'd better extend our visit another day, so we can see a few more of the many things this fascinating city has to offer. Not that we could see them all . . . people

Olvera, a replica of an eighteenth century Mexican street is the place where, in September, 1781, the pueblo of La Nuestra Senora, La Reina de Los Angeles, began as a municipal entity.

Wilshire Boulevard, one of Los Angeles' main thoroughfares, runs through Beverly Hills, one of the most exclusive cities in the world.

The George C. Page Museum near the La Brea tar pits has the reconstructed skeletons of mammoths trapped in the sticky exudate, and perfectly preserved.

An air-conditioned home in sight of the neighboring mountains, sleek horses in an adjoining pasture, and an equally sleek Jaguar purring in the driveway all add up to the good life in San Dimas, a suburb of Los Angeles.

who have lived here all their lives are continually making new discoveries. A little tip from practical experience: if your only requirement is shelter for the night, make it outside of Los Angeles proper, in the suburbs. A little judicious shopping will get you a reasonably priced, nice place to stay: something available in Los Angeles, if at all, only after considerably more shopping and expenditure of valuable time.

We'll sleep in the next morning: no use bucking all that freeway traffic between 6:30 and 9:00 a.m. but when we finally get back to central Los Angeles, we're only a short distance from the small park on Olvera Street where, in 1781, Governor Felipe De Neve founded the city with a nucleus of twelve families of mixed Indian and Negro blood, practically all illiterates: something that arch-rival San Francisco icily claims set the intellectual tenor of Los Angeles for generations to come.

Olvera Street, the heart of this district, was restored in 1931 as a Mexican street typical of the time in which the city was founded. Lined its full length with Mexican shops and restaurants, it draws a constant stream of visitors, an increasing number of whom are Japanese carrying expensive cameras and camcorders. The adjacent mission of La Nuestra Senora de Los Angeles is not only an historical shrine, but also still in active use as a parish church by the local Catholic community.

There is so much to see in Los Angeles that practically any taste can be satisfied. There are guides available to show you anything from the homes of the stars to Forest Lawn Cemetery, where the art of blunting the pangs of bereavement has been honed to a fine art. The motion picture studios also have guided tours, although our cameras are not welcome there, but as is almost always the case, the city itself is the best show. Museums abound, and give the lie to those Los Angeles-haters who sneeringly claim that the city has about as much culture as a Neanderthal. Certainly it is big, brash, often vulgar, and its ghettos can be islands of repression and despair, but it also has a superb vitality, and enclaves of beauty and refinement that are the equal of any other city in America.

Probably the best way to get an idea of the full extent of Los Angeles is to visit Griffith Park toward sundown. The huge 4107 acre park crowns a hill overlooking the city, and from the planetarium at its summit, a panoramic view with its miles and miles of lights spreads out at our feet. As far as the eye can see, clear to the horizon thirty miles or more away the carpet of twinkling lights spreads out in an unbroken pattern delineating the streets and proving, once and for all, that although the metropolitan area may be made up of separate cities, they are all part of the megalopolis that makes up Greater Los Angeles.

The population of Los Angeles keeps growing at an amazing rate while that of other large cities remains static or actually declines. It is true that its famous eye-smarting smog, which hangs over the whole city in a yellowish-gray cloud can, on a bad day, become an acute health hazard, and that may deter some people from moving here. Thousands of others feel that the advantages of living in what many people claim is a wonderful climate and in a city with a host of advantages for an ambitious, hard-working person far outweigh the disadvantages. Three million people can't all be wrong, and the fact that every year more and more people from the winter-ridden sections of the country elect to settle here in the land of eternal Spring is as good an argument as any for its continual growth.

In a city as large and complex as Los Angeles, it is inevitable that all aspects of society, the good as well as the bad, will be represented. Much publicity has been given, of late, to the unenviable fact that Los Angeles has supplanted Miami, Florida, as the drug capitol of the United States. While this is a distinction that the city's most avid booster would just as soon forego, it is nevertheless a fact, and one that the city authorities are preparing to meet head-on.

Miami, twenty years ago, was faced with a problem that is today comparatively new in Los Angeles. When Castro's Marxist government took over Cuba, Miami was almost overwhelmed by a flood of refugees speaking a foreign language and with a set of standards and customs quite at odds with the prevailing American culture. Whole sections of Miami were taken over by refugee Cubans, and Spanish became a necessity for anyone wanting to do business with an increasingly large part of the population. Dire warnings were sounded that this was the end of Miami as an American city, and that the Hispanics would substitute an inferior culture on the city that had given them refuge.

Twenty years later, a large part of those refugees have become good Americans, and added a dash of piquant sauce to the bubbling cauldron that is the American melting-pot. Their sons and daughters have gone to college and speak much better English than they do Spanish, while the older generation has, on the whole, enthusiastically embraced the freedoms and opportunities that were denied them in their native land, and become active, voting members of their adopted country.

Los Angeles faces a similar problem today, but with a few significantly different factors. The flood of immigrants, both legal and illegal, is attracted to Los Angeles by the very factors that make up the character of the city. There are sections of Los Angeles where immigrants can easily live for a whole year without ever speaking a word of English; places where the customs, food, and language are no different than they were in their native Mexico, except that the food is more abundant. Nevertheless, it is inevitable that the pervasive American culture will impinge on their lives, and little by little, leave its mark. The Hispanic youth working as a day laborer on the new home of a wealthy Anglo may be burning with a fierce determination that someday, he too, will have a home like this one, for is this not the land of opportunity?

The big difference is that the Cuban influx was largely of well educated professionals who readily adapted to the customs and language of their new country, while the influx from Mexico, especially the illegals, is largely poor and uneducated. The process of integration will necessarily be slower, but such are the assimilative powers of Los Angeles, that in a generation or two, these may be the leaders of the community, and as good Americans as anyone. The answer, of course, is education, and a significant part of the educational facilities of the city are slanted toward the goal of having young Pépé Gonzalez speak, read, and write English as well as young Billy Smith. The period of transition is the time of the greatest dangers, for in a city as sybaritic as Los Angeles, the temptation to take shortcuts to that pot of gold is understandably strong.

There is no question but that this is the land of the lotus-eaters. The warm, sub-tropical climate, the year-round sunshine, the ready availability of beaches and recreational areas, but most of all the large amount of disposable income available to a generally well-educated, affluent class wedded to the culture of eternal youth all make a hedonistic lifestyle not only possible, but probable. Within the confines of the suburbs ringing Los Angeles, there are people who can easily afford a beautiful home, with stables, the inevitable swimming pool, a Jaguar or two in the garage, and still have enough disposable income to send their sons and daughters to some very expensive colleges. It is quite natural that people given these opportunities to live the good life, Southern California style, will take it.

The temptation to stay awhile and further explore this fascinating city is a strong one, but must be resisted. There is still much of Highway 101 ahead.

The Hollywood Freeway becomes the Ventura Freeway once it has passed Universal City and on its way northward marches through a mixed residential and business environment for over thirty miles before any appreciable open space begins to prevail. Let's take one of the exits leading to a suburban section. Here we find the big reason why so many people happily call this region "home." Large, tree-shaded lots, immaculately clipped lawns, a profusion of flowers, swimming pools everywhere; all the amenities of gracious living. It may entail a daily two hour-long struggle on a crowded freeway, but when one gets home in the evening the beauty that surrounds one can make it all worth while, or so it seems.

When it comes to picking city sites, that old Franciscan, Fra Crespi, was in a class by himself!

Built in 1928 when all other buildings in Los Angeles County were restricted to a height of thirteen stories, City Hall for several decades towered over the rest of Los Angeles. While it is now dwarfed by skyscrapers that have sprung up since the recession of that rule, it still is a very impressive building which has a wonderful view of Los Angeles, smog permitting.

The Bank of California Building is typical of the modern skyscrapers that are being built to supposedly earthquake-proof standards in downtown Los Angeles, dwarfing venerable City Hall and giving the city a look commensurate with its size.

CHAPTER 3

MISSION TRAIL

The pall of smog overhanging the City of Los Angeles begins to fade into the distance as we head northward on the Ventura Freeway toward San Francisco, which is a good day's journey ahead of us if we don't make too many stops, but a good three or more days if we stop to smell some of the flowers along the way. Since we have already determined that we would savor the bites we took out of our large pie, we'd better count on a minimum of three days, or even more: this is the Mission Trail, and there is much to see in the days ahead.

The Franciscan friars who first laid out the Mission Trail would have been envious of our most leisurely rate of progress, for the route we will be traveling is largely the one over which they plodded on sandaled feet between the chain of missions from San Diego to Sonoma. The missions were roughly one day apart, so that at the end of a day's journey, the weary friars could look forward to a good meal, several cheering glasses of wine, and a clean, if somewhat hard bed. We will see several of these missions in our travels along 101, the old El Camino Real, and the example those long ago friars set is still good advice to this day.

Since the missions played such an important part in the development of California, a little background information may help us to better understand the character of the country through which we will be passing. We already know that the initial discoveries of Juan Cabrillo made this country Spanish territory, and that it was not developed until Fra Junipero founded his first mission at San Diego in 1769. It was the first in a chain of nine he was to found before

his wasted body, full of years, honors, and unhealed sores was laid to rest beneath the flagstones of his beloved Mission Carmel.

Fra Junipéro Serra is honored by the state of California with a statue in Statuary Hall, in Washington D.C. where the memories of the men and women who were instrumental in developing their individual states are permanently enshrined, but the general public does not know nearly enough about this indomitable son of St. Francis. We have already mentioned that when he began his California missions, he was a sick old man, but the fact bears repetition if only to emphasize the magnitude of the accomplishments performed by this remarkable man. His church has already conferred the title of "blessed" upon him, the first step toward canonization, but if it had been up to the Indians whom he loved passionately and for whom he dedicated his life, he probably would have had the title conferred upon him during his lifetime. Given the glacial pace at which the Catholic Church today confers sainthood, it may be generations, if ever, before that title is conferred, but history has already dubbed him "The Apostle of California."

In spite of an ulcerated leg which caused him constant pain and which he used too much to ever allow to heal properly, he walked across a good part of the world's toughest obstacle course, Baja California, and many more miles along the trail which we will follow in his footsteps: the Mission Trail, known in his day as El Camino Real.

A large part of the success he and his followers were to enjoy in the foundation of their missions was due to the rigorous training these dedicated men underwent, and the almost complete autonomy they achieved in lands nominally under secular control. As a rule, they were highly cultured men, often the younger sons of prominent Spanish families, trained in the Indian languages they would be using, and knowledgeable in music, architecture, agriculture, irrigation and above all, administration. A secular officer who often crossed swords with the sons of St. Francis describes them as men with "fire in their bellies" and he found out, to his considerable surprise, that the real ruler of Alta California was not the viceroy's representative in Monterey, or even the viceroy himself in Mexico City, but the mild-mannered, soft spoken Franciscan who ran the mission system.

This unique advantage came from the fact that they had the undivided support of the Spanish crown. Those pragmatists in the Escorial soon found out that the system of missions established by the tireless Franciscans were producing docile Indians and prosperous outposts of Spanish civilization far more efficiently than any military outposts or secular pueblo. Charles III was a very intelligent man who seldom argued with success.

The prime reason for establishing a mission was to Christianize the Indians: a very compelling reason in those days of perfervid faith. In order to do that, the Indians had to be weaned from their nomadic ways and made self-sufficient, something they had seldom achieved under their own system even in this land of easy living. The idea was that as soon as they were self-sufficient, the Indians were to receive back the lands their labor had fructified, and they would become loyal, tax-paying subjects of the Spanish crown.

A fine idea, only it didn't work out that way. The California Indians, not by nature a warlike lot, since war required the expenditure of considerable energy, readily adapted to mission life, and found in it a security they had never achieved under their tribal system. The mission was all things to them: home, refuge, hospital, school, granary, and the padres were readily accepted as the new chiefs. The big problem was that even after three generations they saw no reason to change a system that suited them perfectly well, even if their every day activity were governed by the mission bell.

The site of each mission was chosen very carefully, with an eye for expansion, which may help to explain why several of the mission sites grew into large cities. Most of them became quite successful, and very wealthy, with huge herds of cattle, extensive olive groves, vineyards, and stables full of blooded horses. The center of each mission was, of course the church, but next to each church there were quarters for the priests, barracks for the soldiers who served as security guards, and the various shops that made each mission not only a self-sufficient entity, but also a manufacturing center capable of producing a wide variety of useful trade goods. One of the missions, San Juan Capistrano, even had a Catalan forge where local iron ore was converted to pig iron, and from that into a host of useful metal utensils. The school was a very important part of the mission, and while not every student showed a marked aptitude for learning, there were a few who did, and these were meticulously groomed by the alert friars who saw in them the future leaders of their people. The missions even produced a musical prodigy, who, unexplainably denied access to the mission's musical instruments, crafted his own violin from native woods; an instrument that to this day is on display at Mission San Antonio and amazes anyone who knows its history. In short, the mission was an oasis of culture and security in a largely barbaric desert.

Because wine was needed for the sacrifice of the Mass, vineyards were planted at each of the missions, usually to the prolific Mission grape which made up what it lacked in finesse by yielding vast quantities of wine. The California wine industry, now one of the acknowledged leaders in the world, traces its lineage directly to these humble beginnings, and that is the reason why the blessing of the grapes, a custom still honored in some California wineries, is usually done by a Franciscan. Olives, since time immemorial have been associated with vineyards, and these were liberally planted at the missions, where they were pressed for oil, and the residue used as a high-powered cattle feed. Life was good at the missions: the work was hard, but no one ever went hungry, and there was always a glass of wine to celebrate a feast-day or simply to wash down the dust of the day's toil.

The missions were usually planned as an equal sided quadrangle, with the church making up one side of the square, and the additional buildings enclosing the centrally located mission garden, complete with fountain and reflecting pool. The

Probably the world's most photographed tree, the famous Lone Cypress at Point Lobos is not far from Mission Carmel, where Fra Junipéro Serra is interred.

At Mission San Juan Capistrano, a statue of Fra Junipéro Serra, the Apostle of California, stands amidst the ruins of one of the nine missions he founded.

garden was usually planted with flowers and lovingly tended, for these cultured men far from the perfumed gardens of Spain, still longed for the beauty of their homeland. The mission garden was one place, in this wild, beautiful, but often lonely land, where one could walk in the coolness of twilight or dawn, and imagine himself back in Seville.

As the missions prospered, they took in more and more farm and pasture land, so that some of them became huge and very wealthy ranches. The Indians formed a docile workforce, and although they theoretically could leave at any time they so desired, in practice very few did, for the mission way of life soon supplanted the tribal system under which they had previously lived. Some of the later administrators could be at least understood, if not forgiven, if the soldiers were sent out to round up some worker who, after living two generations on mission food, had decided to take an unscheduled vacation at the peak of harvest.

Visitors to the mission, and they were surprisingly numerous, were unanimous in their praise of the hospitality extended to them. A visitor could stay as long as he pleased, and if he should have arrived afoot, the victim of some unfortunate circumstance, was often presented with a fine horse when he finally decided to take his leave. He was, however, expected to attend daily Mass, a requirement that puzzled the many Yankee sailors, mostly Protestants, who made the missions a regular port of call. Most of them complied, feeling that an hour on one's knees was a small price to pay for the pleasant sojourn they were enjoying.

The missions, being fiefs of the Spanish crown, usually had a small complement of resident soldiers; the larger missions, or one adjacent to a presidio, with up to fifteen men under the command of an officer, the smaller ones with six men under the command of a corporal or sergeant. Superb horsemen and outdoorsmen, each man was equipped with a lance, a heavy musket and pistol, a saber, and sundry accessories. For transportation, he had six horses and a mule, as well as unlimited access to the mission's well-stocked stables. The experience of two centuries had proved that the steel corselet of the early conquistadors was too hot: steel conducts heat, and in the sometimes torrid summers of California, had a tendency to parboil even the toughest soldier. Besides, it was discovered that the leather armor that was soon substituted was perfectly adequate

to stop the primitive stone-tipped arrows of the Indians, and was much cooler. A heavy leather apron, reaching down to the knees was used when riding through chapparal brush: the ancestor of the present-day cowboy chaps.

The soldiers assigned to the mission were forced to pay for their own equipment, which meant they took very good care of what was issued to them, and that the more careless ones did many years' duty to pay off their indebtedness. Actually, a mission assignment was "good duty." The Indians were mostly docile, the horses were the best, and life under the guidance of the padres was pleasant, in spite of the calloused knees. Many a soldier with the idea in mind of lightening up future generations of Indians or depleting the generous wine stocks of the missions found out, even before he had a chance to attempt his first transgression, that the iron discipline the Franciscans applied to themselves could also be imposed on their charges. . .and that included many a rough soldier who came back from an interview with a gray-garbed Franciscan with a face to match the color of his superior's clerical robes. Dismissal from the mission service meant either a life on the run as a deserter. . .and the king's arm was notoriously long. . .or a stint of building stone fortifications under the broiling sun of Baja California. Discipline was strict, for both whites and Indians, but under the guidance of men dedicated to the salvation of souls, fair and impartial. For that reason most of them behaved, and many of them, when their tour of duty was completed, returned to the missions as civilian directors. Many of California's oldest and most distinguished families can proudly trace their ancestry back to a "cuirodado," as the leather-clad soldiers were called.

When the Mexican Revolution began in 1810, this presented a dilemma to most of the mission superiors, a dilemma which came to a head in 1821, when the revolution was finally successful. Since the missions were fiefs of the crown, most of the priests were fiercely loyal to the king, and wary of the largely anti-clerical revolutionists who made up the new government. That was one of the reasons used by the victorious rebels to justify their secularization of the missions, which was implemented in 1835. Only one mission, San Juan Bautista, was not completely secularized, and that was because the incumbent priest, a native born Mexican, had no pangs of conscience swearing allegiance to a regime

One of the best preserved of all the missions, Mission San Juan Bautista still serves as a parish church for the local Catholic community. It is the only one of the missions that had three aisles.

composed of his own countrymen. The rest were declared property of the state, and the Franciscans sent packing.

It was a disaster of the first order.

When the era of colonialism ended in Africa after World War II, and the colonies were given their independence, those new countries soon found out that life under native rule was not nearly the Utopia they had been promised, and that white administrators had not been so bad after all. So it was with the missions. Some of them were given as political plums to those who had ardently supported the revolution, others were sold at a fraction of their real worth to those who had greased the right palms, and those that found no new owners were simply abandoned. The new owners, having a vested interest in seeing to it that the priests should never again regain their possessions, became rabidly anti-clerical. The Indians, deprived of the guiding hands of the padres, became beggars, brigands, or the virtual slaves of the arrogant hidalgos who had little or no interest in saving their immortal souls, and soon replaced calloused knees with whip-scarred backs.

The mission churches were abandoned. Stucco peeled off the adobe walls, and in time the elements reduced many of them to muddy ruins. When the Americans took over control of California, those missions which were still the property of the Mexican government were returned to the Catholic Church by presidential decree, but most of them were in ruins, and in few cases have been restored to the glory that was theirs during the hey-day of the mission padres.

We have already briefly visited one mission, San Juan Capistrano, founded by Fra Junipéro Serra in 1776. At one time it was one of the largest missions, with a spacious stone church completed in 1806 and destroyed by earthquake December 12, 1812 during morning Mass with a heavy loss of life. The ruins are still there, with a bell-wall holding four of the original mission bells standing bravely by the side of the wrecked church.

San Juan Capistrano is probably the best known of the missions, mostly because of its punctual swallows which arrive in force on the feast of St. Joseph, March 19, and depart just as punctually on the 23rd of October. How do the swallows know when it's leap year? Only the swallows know, and they aren't telling, but they somehow arrive and depart on those two dates with puzzling regularity, leap year or no leap year. The mission gardens are extensive and have been beautifully restored, while the founder's chapel, the oldest church in California, is still in pretty much in its original state. Fra Serra, who obviously had been given powers usually reserved for a bishop, confirmed 223 people in this church in 1783. The nave is quite narrow, since the roof width was restricted to the length of the available logs used as roof-trusses. We have already mentioned the Catalan forge and the iron-smelting activities which made this mission a center of industry in the middle of a wilderness.

There are several other missions north of Los Angeles and we will visit any that are not too far off our path. Actually, since the road pretty well follows the old mission trail, we will not miss too many, so let's get on our way.

The freeway to Ventura is mostly past a solid wall of urban development, with a few orange groves and bean-fields as yet resisting the tide of urban encroachment. Is it because they are profitable? Hardly! Not as agricultural enterprises, that is, but the value of those fields is doubling and tripling every year as the tide of urban growth laps at their boundaries. As long as they are in crops, they pay taxes as agricultural land, so the crops are dutifully harvested, even if the labor costs more than the crops bring in. At the rate those lands are appreciating, the owner can well afford to take a temporary loss while his nest-egg grows.

We catch sight of the ocean again, with oil-derricks incongruously sprouting from salt water. Five miles south of Carpinteria, a splash of green at the bottom of a sere mountain catches our eye. Can it possibly be? Those big leaves look like banana plants, but here? In California?

Strangely enough, that is exactly what it is: the world's northernmost banana plantation. Actually, there are some farther north, in the Azores, but that doesn't really count because they are on an island surrounded by a tropical sea, while these are growing vigorously in a sub-tropical climate. It is true that they are in a micro-climate next to a large heat-reservoir, the Pacific Ocean, but they are still quite an achievement. The plantation is carefully nurtured by partners Paul Turner and Doug Richardson who say the reason they started this plantation is that they like bananas, and the only way they can get the flavors they prefer is to grow their own.

Whatever reason, the seven acres of carefully tended fruit is here and is rapidly becoming a tourist attraction as people find out that the small but extremely tasty fruit tastes the way God intended a banana to taste. It takes eighteen months for the fruit to mature, as opposed to twelve in the tropics, but the happy owners, surveying their plastic-wrapped bunches well protected from bugs and bruising, feel the wait is worthwhile, an opinion apparently shared by the visitors who invariably buy a few bunches to take back home, as, if nothing else, a wonderful conversation piece.

In a few more miles we arrive in Santa Barbara, as gorgeous a city as ever graced a beautiful site. Situated on a beach between the Santa Ynez mountains and the Pacific, it is the home of eighty thousand happy boosters who are confident that they have the best possible blend of urban and nearby rural life. They just may be right: the weather is wonderful the year round, the site is smog-free and the wide, sandy beaches are in year-round use.

Santa Barbara is the site of the Queen of the missions, Mission Santa Barbara, founded in 1786 by that indefatigable founder of missions, Fra Serra. It is a twin-belfried, dazzling white church, flanked by the usual shaded walk containing the mission buildings. The ubiquitous fountain in this case is at the side of the church and is a much-photographed part of the mission complex. The church is in active use by one of the Catholic parishes in Santa Barbara, and is therefore in a good state of repair. In every mission that we have visited, and this one is no exception, there is a fountain and an enclosed mission garden with lots of flowers, apparently an attempt to recreate a bit of Spanish homeland on the part of the missionaries. Every decent Spanish home has a central court, usually surrounded by a wall, where the members of the family can relax in privacy. It would probably embarrass the good fathers to point out to them that this is probably part of their Moorish heritage, for in those homes, the most carefully guarded, most private part was the harem, and it invariably had a fountain and lots of flowers.

Our next detour from 101, is along SR 246, ostensibly to visit another mission, Santa Ynez, founded in 1804. Obviously the work that Fra Serra started devolved into capable hands, for this one was founded after he had been laid to rest, and in a short time became one of the wealthiest of the missions, with a cattle herd of over 12,000 head. Beautifully restored, it still serves as a parish church for the Catholics of the Santa Ynez Valley.

To get to Mission Santa Ynez, we had to pass through a village which looks as though it had been transplanted lock, stock and barrel from Denmark. The architecture, the store fronts even a couple of windmills recreate the feeling of a Danish town so perfectly that we should start checking to see if our passports are in order. That is exactly what the inhabitants of Solvang intended, and they would probably give each other a complimentary wink that the ambience they have created is so good that it could deceive someone to whom Denmark is a fond memory. The town was founded in 1911 when three Danish educators, looking for a place where they could found a town with solidly Danish roots and values saw the Santa Ynez Valley and decided this is where they would found a community where the customs and traditions of their homeland would be preserved. They succeeded, although today Solvang (which means "Sunny Field" in Danish) is only 20% of Danish descent. In feeling however, all partake of the same spirit that makes everyone Irish on St. Patrick's day. In Solvang, everyone is Danish at heart, every day of the year, a feeling which does much in this sparkling clean community to keep up the appearance of an Old World town transplanted intact to the New World.

Let's stop here. I have friends in Solvang, and since we have time for only one stop, let's visit with the prettiest one. If ever I came through Solvang and didn't stop to say "Hello" and have a glass of Carlsberg with Peggy Evans, she'd stomp all over me the next time we met, and I don't want that beautiful big hunk of a Viking mad at me or my friends.

The proud owner of the Danish Inn, one of the finest restaurants in Solvang, she is one of the town's most avid boosters, and the best exemplification of Scandinavian hospitality I have ever met. The whole town, for that matter, is a reflection of the good food, good beer, and buxom blondes that have made Denmark a tourist's favorite for years. Here, you don't even need a passport, and the Danish breakfast you can get in Solvang for under four dollars is hearty enough to carry you through the whole day. You wouldn't want to do that, though: the whole place is an adventure in good eating, pleasant company, and the kind of surroundings that fairly begs "Stay a while." An added incentive is that the monstrous

Mission Santa Barbara, the "Queen of the Missions," has seen a good sized city grow up around it: proof that those old time Franciscans chose their mission sites extremely well.

The Madonna Inn at San Luis Obispo must be seen to be believed. Largely constructed of huge rocks, it is probably the world's most solidly constructed motel.

The decor of the Madonna Inn has been decried by critics as "An explosion in a factory manufacturing pink paint." Those same critics probably intentionally overlook the fact that the place is filled to capacity every moment that it is open.

tabs for food and lodging to which we unwillingly became accustomed in the large cities are conspicuous here mostly by their absence. We could live here three days for what we pay for one in Los Angeles. . . and live better at that. A wonderful idea, but let's pass that one up this time. We can always come back when our cholesterol count is down enough that we could stand a few days of the superb Danish cooking and really soak up the hospitality Solvang dispenses so readily.

When we get back to 101, we might as well cross over the highway because for a hundred miles we have been seeing signs touting Buellton and Pea-soup Anderson. This is another Scandinavian institution and one we can hardly afford to pass up. Yes, the pea-soup is as good as the ads imply, and it's only a mile off 101, a very small detour to smell another one of the flowers along the way.

Fueled by an euphoric pea-soup high and at peace with the world, we continue northward past an Air Force base dedicated to keeping the whole world that way. This is Vandenberg Air Force Base, where many of the United States' long range missiles are tested, either launched out over the broad Pacific, or into spatial orbit. We can't promise you we'll see a hundred-foot-long "bird" ascending on its pillar of fire, but it does sometimes happen, and we may get lucky, especially if we tarry in the neighborhood a few days.

We've come inland a little bit, but at Pismo Beach we see the ocean again, and in a highly picturesque setting. Here, 101 dives inland toward our next stop, the famed Madonna Inn at San Luis Obispo.

The Madonna Inn is the brainchild and hobby of a remarkable man, Alex Madonna, founder of one of California's largest construction companies, and a man who has had much to do with 101: his firm built a large part of it. A self-made multi-millionaire, he was often confronted, in his many travels away from home with inferior motels at inflated prices, so the idea of building a nice motel for nice people àt a fair price began to grow in his mind. He was at the time building a thirty-mile long canal, and the construction entailed the use of many large rocks, some of which were obviously surplus as the project neared completion. Since he must dispose of those rocks, and he had the heavy equipment necessary to move them, he decided to build his motel out of rock, using his surplus as a beginning.

He told me this story himself, while I was appreciatively demolishing one of his superb steaks. When he swung the first huge rock into position, using a heavy construction crane, the load was almost as heavy as the crane and the crane started tipping over. Alex quickly dropped the rock, and where it landed, "That" he said "was where the first room was built."

Madonna Inn is something that must be seen to be believed. Undoubtedly one of the prime tourist attractions in the whole length of 101, it is a fantasy of shapes and colors that seems to have grown with no apparent rhyme or reason but is still certainly the most solidly built motel in existence. Hundred ton boulders in the walls of a room are common, and some of them top two hundred tons: big enough that it took two gigantic D9 Caterpillar tractors straining at full power to move them into position. Building a motel out of irregularly shaped rocks is unique enough, but that's only the beginning. For one thing, the stultifying monotony of shape and layout which makes one hotel room like several thousand others is conspicuous by its absence here: no two rooms in the two-hundred room inn are alike, and some are unlike any other motel room anywhere in the world. One famous room can be entered only by crawling through a rocky tunnel, and the decor is prehistoric cave man, with a few modern touches of luxury, of course. Several rooms have shower stalls of rough-hewn rock and no discernible shower-heads. Turn the fixture, and water spurts out at you from all directions out of the rocky wall. Needless to say, these rooms are prime favorites with honeymooners and are solidly booked for months ahead.

The decor of each room is, to say the least, unusual. The room in which I stayed had a western motif: the king-sized bed was on the bed of a wagon complete with wheels, and the whole room was full of antiques, quite a few of them, to an eye trained in evaluating European inlaid furniture, worth many thousands of dollars. That is nothing unusual: most of the rooms are furnished with antiques, some of them priceless. Does this present a theft problem? Very seldom, and should one ever be found to be missing by the alert staff, a polite request for its return is usually sheepishly honored. If that doesn't work, the bill that is sent to the borrower is sufficiently authoritative to merit prompt attention. Colors are as wild as an explosion in a paint factory, but run strongly to Madonna Pink, the favorite color of Alex and his lovely wife, Phyllis.

Strange as this may sound, the effect is pleasing, even fascinating, and as the saying goes, the proof of the pudding is in the eating: the Madonna Inn is always at least 90% booked up just on advance reservations, and the rest is usually taken up by people who may have even booked a room in adjacent motels, just in case a reservation might be canceled.

Alex Madonna is one of the luckiest, or maybe I should say smartest men I know. He has his work, his lovely wife who was his high-school sweetheart, a talented, devoted family, and his motel which started out as a hobby and became a good-sized business enterprise. The mostly pine coffee-shop, where he has his special booth, is his command post. Armed with an ever-present telephone, he keeps an eye on things, supervises his 257 employees, every one of whom he knows by name, and makes sure that every aspect of the place lives up to the national reputation for excellence it has achieved. He is especially proud. . .justifiably. . .of the meat served in his restaurant. "We grow our own," he says, and he does, on one of his twenty ranches, one of which has over 12,500 head of cattle. He and Phyllis meet for a morning cup of coffee and may design a new room with some particularly outrageous bit of decoration. Maybe it would be more accurate to say "over decoration" for the decor of Madonna Inn is so blatantly rococo that by sheer force of overkill, it becomes attractive. Not all critics agree. "Tarzania Terrible" one will say. "Anaheim Awful" another will mutter. Those critics should be reminded of a 99% occupancy rate, and the fact that some people have had to wait a year or more to book some popular room. You don't argue with that kind of success, and no one gets more fun out of confusing the critics of his personal gold-mine than Alex gets out of his.

San Luis Obispo, the site of another of Fra Serra's missions, is a pretty little city generally regarded as the northern tip of Southern California. The mission is practically in the center of town, further proof that those old Franciscans had a pretty canny eye for building sites, since so many of their missions have blossomed into cities. The mission is very well restored, and is in active use as the local Catholic parish church. The original decorations, done by Indian converts using locally obtained pigments are particularly notable, and do much to induce a feeling of continuity with the early days of the mission.

This stop is definitely one of our flowers, as is the delightful town of Paso Robles, a half hour or so to

the north. If we happen to be hungry, the Paso Robles Inn is a nice place to stop. We should take time to stroll through the beautifully laid out grounds, a relic of the inn designed by Stanford White, which was destroyed by fire but rebuilt as closely as possible to the spirit of the original plan.

This is indeed the Mission Trail: we have another one ahead of us at San Miguel. When this mission was secularized, a nucleus of devout converts saw to it that the mission church was not allowed to fall into ruins, as so many of them were, so that today one can still stroll through the mission gardens or attend services in a mission that is practically unchanged from the days when the congregation was mostly Indians.

One of the most interesting, largest, and best preserved missions will necessitate a twenty-six mile detour off 101, but it is worth it. This is the Mission San Antonio de Padua which, unlike most of the other missions, still has a Franciscan community serving it, and is not near a town. We leave 101 at Bradley and take G18 toward Fort Hunter Ligget. At an Army check-point on the outskirts of the sprawling reservation, a polite MP gives us directions to the mission, which is just outside the western border of the fort.

Mission San Antonio de Padua was founded July 14, 1777 when that tireless founder of missions, Fra Junipéro Serra hung a mission bell in a grove of oak trees and with its ringing brought a crowd of curious Indians out of the underbrush. This mission was all things to all men: school, church, hospital, grist-mill, winery, tannery, bakery, but above all, a reliable supplier of food and security. Located in a favorable spot at the foot of the Coast Range, it soon grew to be a very prosperous and populous mission; a favorite visiting spot of Yankee sailors, as the carved ship figure-heads they left as "Thank You" mementoes will testify.

When secularization was implemented in 1835, San Antonio found no buyer, and was abandoned. Enough of the Indian converts stayed, tending its fields, that when the emaciated body of a Franciscan who had died of starvation at Mission Soledad was brought here by Indians, they were able to give it honorable burial under the flagstones of the church.

A presidential decree signed by Abraham Lincoln restored the mission to the Franciscans, who still have an active chapter here. It owes its present state of excellent restoration to the generosity of William

(Overleaf) Solvang, a scant three miles off Highway 101, is such a good re-creation of a Danish village in America, that one keeps feeling his inside pocket to make sure the precious passport is still there. Don't worry! English is spoken, and the natives are friendly. . .to a fault!

Randolph Hearst, who had a hunting lodge nearby and who, taking an interest in the restoration of the mission, established a trust fund to that end which to this day helps with the upkeep of this bit of California's early history. If you are a mission buff, or even if you are not, this one is worth the detour. Since we are seeing 101 together, this is one flower we are not only going to smell, but admire at length. It is worth it.

Returning to 101, we have a different kind of flower to smell. The highway passes through a basin where a hundred or more oil-pumps are doing a rhythmic dance, moving in slow arcs as they pump out the liquid wealth of San Ardo oil field, discovered in 1948. Since a county road passes through the heart of the operation, we can get a good look at an actively producing petroleum facility without trespassing on private land, although if we should like to have a closer look, the company authorities are very gracious about granting permission. The heavy crude comes out of the ground at 80°, and partly for greater mobility, is boosted to 300° in specially designed flow-houses which also inject super-heated steam into the ground to facilitate pumping. A strict regard to ecological consideration ensures that relations with nearby residents remain amicable.

We are now at the bottom edge of the Salinas Valley, the nation's salad bowl. It is really a gorgeous, very fertile area bounded on the left by wooded mountains and on the right, ten miles or so away by a range of rounded hills. Blessed with warm, moist climate and soil of amazing fertility, it grows a large part of the lettuce, cabbage, and broccoli that winds up on the nation's dinner table, clear to the East Coast.

While growing conditions in the Salinas Valley are generally very favorable, it also is renowned as the home of the agriculturists who are probably the industry's greatest gamblers. Because some crops, notably lettuce can be grown to maturity here in a matter of weeks, fortunes are made. . .or lost. . .in a very short time. The lettuce farmer who puts in a couple thousand acres of the succulent green stuff is betting that when his crop comes to maturity anywhere from three to six weeks from planting, there will be a market for his produce, because once it is ready for harvest, that's when you harvest it. If it should mature too soon or too late, he can be stuck with a few thousand tons of very nice salad material

that no one wants, and a first rate tragedy, because today's finicky buyers will not accept a substandard crop. I distinctly remember the sick feeling I experienced in seeing hundreds of acres of beautiful cabbages being disked into the soil as green fertilizer, and the glum owner explaining to me that his crop had matured at a time when market conditions were such that he couldn't recoup even the cost of the labor necessary to harvest it.

Was he downhearted? Only temporarily. The new crop would be seeded within days, and if it matured at the right time, he would not only recoup his losses but make enough profit so that he could survive at least one more disaster. That is a farmer's life in the Salinas Valley, but I also noticed that most of their wives were driving brand new Cadillacs.

A recent development in this area is the planting of thousands of acres of vineyards, all of choice varietal grapes, as the farmers of this area decided to get in on the wine boom that was sweeping the nation in the early 1980s. They may have made their move too late; a vineyard takes five years to become actively productive, and the wine boom is flattening out, at least for the average quality table wine. Nevertheless, the new vineyards are there, and not far behind are the facilities for vinting the bountiful harvest that this fertile valley will predictably produce.

We make another detour at Soledad to view the mission of Nuestra Senora de la Soledad. It is about a five mile detour from 101, situated way out in the country. The church and some outbuildings have been restored as a museum, but the shop area, built of adobe, has deteriorated into mounds of muddy rubble and probably will never be restored to its original condition.

We are now in a region of rolling hills, liberally covered with oaks, and presenting a very appealing landscape. 101 is still a busy, four-lane highway, but the atmosphere has undergone a subtle change and is now definitely rural. We have left Southern California and its development.

Our last mission stop is at San Juan Bautista, a short two-mile jog off 101. This mission is notable in that it has been continuously staffed by Franciscans since its inception in 1797. The largest of the mission churches, it is the only one with three aisles and nine bells, cast in Mexico, three of which are still in use to summon the faithful to Mass. The mission gardens are particularly attractive and the church itself has attractive decorations done long ago by Indian artists. Since this church, alone among all the missions, was never completely secularized, it is in a wonderful state of preservation compared to most of the other missions, and is a worthy ending to our mission tour. There are more missions, and some day we may see them all, clear up to Sonoma, but this is the last one we shall visit along 101.

It is only fair to mention that beautiful as 101 is, it cedes its crown of beauty to the world-famous U.S. 1, which skirts the coast from Carmel to San Luis Obispo, and provides some of the most outstanding vistas in the world. The area it serves was long an almost inaccessible wilderness, the haven of hermit types who had no use for civilization and sought to get away from it in the fastnesses of the Big Sur country. It is still pretty wild, especially in its remote canyons, but it also has some really fancy restaurants and resorts along its scenic 110 mile or so length. If wild seascapes, incredible vistas, and constant surprises are what you seek, and you don't mind a narrow, twisting road, often blasted out of a sheer cliff with a frightening drop to the ocean only a few feet away, then you've found it here. At its southern end, you pass the incredible Casa Grande, William Randolph Hearst's grandiose love-nest in the wilderness, which is now a state park. As an example of what unlimited money can build, it is in a class by itself and well worth the half-day or so it takes to even begin to explore it. At the junction of U.S. 1 at San Luis Obispo, you can catch up with us by turning northward: our trip has been slowed considerably by our inspection of numerous missions along the Mission Trail.

From Gilroy north, the highway is increasingly fringed with urban development until we reach San José, when the development becomes a solid wall and continues all the way to San Francisco. San José formerly was the site of the most productive agricultural area in California, but as so often happens, people drawn to an area because of its natural beauty almost inevitably destroy that beauty by their very presence and numbers. The Santa Clara Valley was inexorably paved over and became a very large city, with all the amenities of a large city, it is true, but with only faint echoes of the natural beauty that formerly made this area so outstanding. The mission of Santa Clara stands on the grounds of Santa Clara University, but we will leave it up to you to explore the many nice features of the San José area on your own. We're too anxious to cover the fifty miles or so of urban development that leads us to our next destination, San Francisco.

In the Salinas Valley, the nation's salad bowl, mechanized handling of the broccoli crop speeds the job.

A good share of the nation's lettuce is grown in the fertile Salinas Valley. Fortunes can be made. . .or lost, overnight in this most volatile of all agribusinesses.

Hoover Tower, the well-known symbol of Stanford University, soars over a prestigious educational institution. Developments engendered at this seat of intellectual ferment are largely responsible for the unprecedented growth of the electronic industry along the corridor that is known as Silicon Valley.

BAGHDAD BY THE BAY

With the possible exception of New Orleans, no city in the United States has the mystique of the one we are approaching as we proceed northward on U.S. 101. San José is behind us, then a busy international airport and Candlestick Park, until finally, around a bend in the freeway a fairyland vision of soaring towers comes into view, painted golden by the rays of a setting sun; San Francisco, the Golden, Baghdad by the Bay.

The journalist who coined that phrase certainly had his finger on the pulse of the place, for if ever a city were to live up to the fantasies of a modern-day Arabian Nights, that city is San Francisco. Blessed with a magnificent location, a salubrious climate which forgives all but the wildest excesses, and just about every advantage a beneficent Nature can bestow, it was destined from the very beginning to become one of the great cities of the world; a destiny it has fulfilled beyond its founders' wildest dreams. For a century and a half, it has been a Mecca for the adventuresome, the creative, the imaginative mind; the haven of those in whom the wine of life courses like a molten torrent, for in this city by the bay, they have found a place where they can live their lives within the limits imposed only by their imaginations or a very liberal interpretation of common law.

There is no doubt whatever that San Francisco Bay is what geologists call a drowned valley. There is, however, quite a bit of dissent as to when this happened. Many geologists are reluctant to admit that any significant geological event could have happened in the last few hundred years, completely ignoring the fact that the catastrophic earthquake that rattled India in 1762 caused sixty miles of shoreline to slide into the ocean. It is much more convenient to assign some date far into the dim past to any event that could have significantly changed the face of a region. So it is with San Francisco Bay.

These geologists usually assign an age of from 40,000 to 15,000 years ago for the formation of San Francisco Bay, the later time corresponding to the retreat of the glaciers in the latest Ice Age. While San Francisco is too far south to have been affected by the great continental ice sheets pushing down from Canada, it is well within the reach of glaciers crawling down from the Sierra Nevada. Digging a bay as large as San Francisco's, while a really impressive job of earth-moving, is well within the capabilities of a large glacier. The break in the coastal hills, however, is not the type of feature a glacier usually creates, but does enlarge.

There is another theorem, one which would explain why Cabrillo, who sailed past this coast in 1542, Sir Francis Drake in 1578, and Sebastian Viscaino in 1602 apparently never found the Golden Gate and the bay behind it. Drake especially, who spent considerable time at Drake's Bay, only fourteen miles north of the entrance to San Francisco Bay in his exploration of what he termed "New Albion" would not have missed the potential of the bay had he ever seen it. His journal states that he climbed Mt. Tamalpais on a clear day to survey the country, and a geographical feature of the magnitude of San Francisco Bay could hardly have escaped his notice. Although he may have been a black-hearted freebooter, he was also a skilled seaman and navigator, and the prospect of securing an anchorage for his beloved queen such as this one, where all navies of the world could comfortably ride at anchor, would have been irresistible.

When Gaspar de Portola discovered San Francisco Bay on his city-founding voyage of 1769, the Indians told him a story that would explain why his may have been the first white man's eyes to look upon the bay. According to the Indian legend, the area where the bay now stands, within the last 150 years, had been a fertile, wooded valley. Then a catastrophic earthquake shook the land, dropping the valley hundreds of feet and creating a monstrous crack in the coastal hills through which the ocean poured for several days and created a new inland sea: San Francisco Bay. Cabrillo, Drake, and Viscaino could not have seen something that simply was not there at the time.

When I first heard this story, I took it with the proverbial grain of salt, but in the name of professional objectivity, I felt I should check it out. After all, the area bestrides the San Andreas fault, and the events the Indians described so vividly and in such detail are all geologically possible. Consultations with professional geologists were a bit more confusing. Some supported the usually accepted theorem that the bay was a drowned valley that was submerged at the end of the latest Ice Age, but others confirmed that there was a growing body of data that suggested that the Indians had not been smoking too much of the local cannabis when they told Cabrillo their story. For one thing, the delta of the Sacramento River is not nearly as large as it should be if it had been pouring into the bay for 15,000 years. Was it commensurate with 300 years? No one would make a definitive statement, but it was easy to see that a good number of them leaned, at least in private, to the theorem that San Francisco Bay was geologically an infant.

Whether the bay is 300 years old or 30,000 is not as important as the fact that it is there, a perfect setting for the gem that is San Francisco. Gaspar de Portola, the white discoverer of the bay, was undeniably gallant, valorous, and handsome, but he must also have been amazingly stupid for the real value of what he discovered apparently never dawned on him. It was not until 1775 that a Spanish ship under the command of Juan Manuel de Ayala breasted the ebbing tide of the Golden Gate and cast

anchor within the confines of the bay. Two months or so after a group of dissident English colonists on the other side of the continent had proclaimed a new nation, a group of Spanish colonists from Monterey established themselves on the tip of the peninsula. The Presidio of San Francisco was founded on September 17, 1776, and on October 9, the ubiquitous Fra Junipéro Serra briskly ringing a mission bell announced the first Mass in the newly founded Mission de San Francisco de Asis. The mission, later renamed Mission Dolores, is still there, part of our Mission Trail.

For all of its obvious commercial possibilities, the growth of Yerba Buena as the settlement was then known, was at a snail's pace. This was mostly due to the policy of the Spanish authorities which favored their own enterprises above all other. Since many of the most energetic hide and tallow traders who were carrying on a brisk trade with the missions farther south were not Spanish, this tended to make Yerba Buena pretty much ignored as a trading post, but as word of the snug harbor and its limitless potential spread, it was inevitable that outside interest would be aroused. In fact, the United States, alerted to the bay's commercial possibilities by Yankee traders, tried unsuccessfully to buy it from Mexico in 1835, even though the settlement then consisted only of a hundred people and a collection of miserable hovels. When, renamed San Francisco, it finally came under American domination in 1847, there were only 800 people there, and the shacks were still miserable.

As in so many other western towns, the magic word that changed this comatose little hamlet into a bustling city was. . .**GOLD**.

There is no doubt that the word was magical; at least it emptied this sleepy little village in a matter of hours as practically every male and not a few females headed for the American River and the opportunity of becoming millionaires. San Francisco did not remain empty for long, as word of the discovery reached the East Coast and the frenzy of the Gold Rush of 1849 picked up steam. Soon the bay was alive with the masts of hundreds of sailing ships as hordes of gold-seekers poured through the town on their way to the gold fields.

''Poured through'' is a very good way of stating this historical fact. Precious few of the 40,000 who arrived by sea or the 30,000 who came overland stayed. Soon the bay became a solid mass of deserted

The Transamerica Tower, at first ridiculed for its unconventional architecture, has become a symbol of San Francisco almost as well-known as the Golden Gate Bridge or the famous cable cars.

ships as their crews departed en masse, leaving their ships unattended.

The real gold in California was garnered not by the gold-seekers who panned the chilly waters of the American River and its tributaries, but by the entrepreneurs who stayed in San Francisco and supplied the prospectors. Eggs sold for a dollar apiece, bacon for twenty-five dollars a pound, and flour for whatever the traffic would bear. Paper money lost all its value: everything was keyed to that elusive yellow dust that was garnered with so much labor and squandered so riotously in the flesh-pots that blossomed overnight in San Francisco. Downtown real estate sold for prices that would have been considered respectable up to a decade ago, lying, cheating, and swindling became the order of the day, and fortunes were made and lost on the turn of a card. San Francisco can justly claim a youth that, to put it kindly, must be called colorful. It can also be said that the future character of the city was formed in those raucous days and nights. A large portion of the men manning the gold fields were young and single, at least at heart, and San Francisco was the last place where they could taste "civilization" before they departed for the incessant labor of the gold-fields, and the first place where they could celebrate when they returned, occasionally with their deerskin pokes bulging with heavy metal dust. A man could be excused if, after several months of bone-wrenching labor he returned to town wealthy, and in a mood for a little celebration.

The big problem was that celebrating "a little" just was not in keeping with the character that San Francisco was developing. Already, the idea was forming that anything worth doing was to be done only one way, and that was full blast. And of course, wherever gold was present in quantity, there were also human vultures who, hoping to pick up more than a little of that precious dust, were ready to pander to every human weakness, and even invent and make available a few new ones. Soon, San Francisco was an armed camp where murder and robbery were so common they were not even reported, and what little authority there was became so overwhelmed by the flood of crime and corruption that in effect, it ceased to exist. A gang of Australian criminals, the Sydney Ducks, moved into town and established a hierarchy of crime until, in desperation, the more responsible elements in town organized a vigilance committee whose avowed purpose it was to clean up the city.

The tolling of a fire bell was the signal that brought hundreds of heavily armed men to a central meeting hall and sent the committee into action. The organized gangs had already been given a choice: get out of town by sundown or be the guest of honor at a well-organized party featuring hempen neckties. Now the trial of one of those criminals who had been warned and had chosen to sneer at the warning was about to begin. The charge was read, and the defendant given a chance to prove his innocence, which usually involved considerable very imaginative verbiage. The committee then consulted amongst themselves and a verdict reached. If the verdict was "Guilty" the action was immediate and without frills; a rope was swung from the nearest stout projecting beam and the defendant summarily hanged. No appeal, no stay of execution, and no lawyers getting rich on legal fees. Crude, by modern standards, but it had some redeeming virtues: the men to whom it was applied richly deserved their fate, and the rate of recidivism was zero. Modern judicial systems could well learn a lesson from the Committee of Twelve, for with the threat of swift, uncompromising retaliation for serious crime, the crime rate dropped dramatically and San Francisco became a place where decent people could lead a reasonably peaceful life.

It was still pretty much a frontier town, with all the problems attendant to rapid growth, but by 1859 San Francisco was established as the metropolis of the Pacific Coast and growing at an astonishing rate. Paved streets were still in the offing, but already some grandiose mansions were being built as the Mother Lode millionaires came back to town and eventually settled down to what passed for respectability in those days. Corruption in politics became a way of life, and only the threat of reviving the vigilantes kept crime in check. With sudden wealth came a demand for the amenities the wealthy take for granted, and soon San Francisco could boast of superb French restaurants and shops selling the latest in Paris fashions, delayed a year or so by a trip around Cape Horn. Travel to the East Coast was a major journey, involving as it did either a stormy passage around South America or an equally perilous crossing of the Isthmus of Panama, then a snake-infested quagmire. Overland travel to the East Coast was even more perilous. The trip was of several months' duration through Indian-infested lands, for

(Overleaf) *The famed Golden Gate Bridge is awe inspiring from any angle, but viewed from the heights to the west of the bridge, especially at a time when day is dying and night is born, it is a never to be forgotten sight.*

even the well-traveled Santa Fe Trail was not completely safe until the turn of the century. Still, a merchant class was emerging that could afford grand pianos, elaborate gowns for their wives, a per capita consumption of fresh oysters that was legendary, and well-stocked wine cellars. The character of San francisco was growing into a well-defined way of life: grab the opportunities life gives you, and live life like a cavalry charge.

If the Gold Rush of 1849 gave San Francisco its first impetus; the silver boon of the 60s and 70s is what kept it going and made it into a modern city. The Comstock Lode alone poured three hundred million dollars into the area, much of which was reinvested into building a city which by 1880 could justly claim to be the social, financial, and cultural center of the West. By that time, San Francisco was know from Mexico to Canada as "The City."

Rudyard Kipling, on visiting The City in the 1890s remarked that "San Francisco is a mad city, inhabited for the most part by perfectly insane people whose women are of a remarkable beauty." Arch-rival Los Angeles, stung by San Francisco's taunts about its illiterate beginning, is fond of remarking "Of course their women are beautiful. Their mothers had to be if they were to be successful in their ancient profession."

There is considerable truth in the taunt, for in the early days when women were scarce, a blind eye could be turned to their former profession as long as they behaved once they were safely married to wealthy and successful men. Nowadays, if it is not fashionable, at least it is not a social disaster to be able to trace one's ancestry to a women whose chief assets when she landed in San Francisco was "a remarkable beauty" and the willingness to share that beauty with lonely men laden with gold dust.

The event that shaped San Francisco's destiny and still hangs like a threatening cloud over the city began at 5:13 a.m. April 18, 1906: a date engraved indelibly on the mind of any true San Franciscan. The San Andreas Fault, one of the greatest geological faults in the world, runs perilously close to San Francisco, and when its accumulated forces were at last released, San Francisco as it then existed was doomed. The earth shuddered convulsively, then heaved and split in successive shocks; elaborate stone fronts crashed into the streets, huge cracks appeared, breaking the water mains, and the fires that immediately broke out burned almost all that was left standing. The mansions of the great, all except the brownstone Flood Mansion atop Nob Hill tumbled down around their owners' ears and thousands of people screamed in terror as their beloved city was reduced to rubble in a matter of minutes.

The fires that raged uncontrolled till April 21 reduced over 800 blocks of San Francisco to smoking ruins, with only a solitary building here and there escaping the inferno. Whole blocks were dynamited to stop the flames, placarded bodies of looters swung from tilting lamp-posts, and in Golden Gate Park masses of homeless people huddled under makeshift shelters and prayed for rain. It came on April 21, but by that time four-fifths of San Francisco was in ashes.

Like the legendary phoenix, The City rose from its ashes, bigger and better than ever. Many of the town-houses that give San Francisco its distinctive air were built between 1906 and 1910, and by that time the traces of the earthquake and fire had become symbols of civic pride; honored scars that said that although The City had been grievously hurt in body, its spirit was not only intact, but having been tempered in the fire, was more indomitable than ever. Actually, this rebirth was nothing new to the city; it was only on a much larger scale. At least six other fires had wiped out the city, and each time they had been seized upon as excuses to improve the city as it was rebuilt. True, the first two fires were in the boom-town period and could only be regarded as blessings, removing as they did a pestilential array of wooden shacks that could only be improved by burning.

This last disaster had leveled not shacks but a proud city, and rebuilding it to an even better level was a task that would have deterred anyone but a San Franciscan, this in spite of an ominous and well-known threat. To this day, people who build in San Francisco realize they are building atop one of the earth's most active and dangerous geological faults: the dividing line between two continental plates that must inevitably some day release their accumulated strains in another disastrous earthquake that would make the world's most powerful nuclear weapon seem like a Chinese New Year firecracker by comparison. It is not a question of "Will it come?" but rather of "When will it come?"

At least a partial answer to this question came at 5:04 P.M. October 17, 1989, when an earthquake measuring 7.1 on the Richter scale shook the Bay area, and in fifteen seconds caused an estimated seven and a half billion dollars in damage. At around five hundred million dollars per second, this is unquestionably the most expensive natural disaster to ever hit the United States.

Unlike the 1906 quake which rumbled through San Francisco like a thousand freight trains, this one was silent, and in that very factor was eerily sinister. Thousands of fans at Candlestick Park, ready to watch the third game of the World Series between the San Francisco Giants and the Oakland Athletics, quietly filed out, some clutching souvenir bits of masonry that had fallen from the upper tiers, to become part of the most monumental traffic jam in The City's history: the freeway between the park and San Francisco, had become a ten-mile-long parking lot—not a single car was moving.

Downtown, the skyscrapers of the financial district were disgorging their usual crowds of office workers, and these were treated to a terrifying sight: huge buildings swaying like trees in a high wind as the titanic forces unleashed by the earth's moving crustal plates sought to bring down buildings that had been built to withstand just such a disaster. Electricity to a large part of the city was cut off, but the buildings of the downtown area fulfilled the promises of their builders, and while they swayed a lot, none fell.

Other parts of the city were not as fortunate. The Marina District, down by Fisherman's Wharf, consisting mainly of posh apartments built on filled in land, shook like a huge bowl of Jello, and many buildings collapsed, trapping their occupants in heaps of rubble. Broken gas mains fed spectacular fires that lightened up the darkened city and in a few hours destroyed over a dozen structures in what had been one of the most desirable and affluent sections of San Francisco.

Bad as this was, it paled in comparison to the devastation that hit the lifeline between San Francisco and Oakland, the Bay Bridge. A mile long section of the double-tiered approach on the Oakland side collapsed, with the top deck dropping thousands of tons of concrete slabs and twisted steel onto the cars of the lower deck, smashing them as though they had been fragile toys. Frantic and often heroic rescue operations began immediately but the devastation was so complete that few thought there would be any survivors.

The spirit that has always animated the inhabitants of the Bay Area really became apparent in the next few days. Hundreds of volunteers toiled at tasks they could never have been induced to do for mere money. The rubble was gradually cleared away, and when a tough old longshoreman was pulled alive out of the wreckage of Interstate 880 after having been interred for four days, the people took it as a sign that everything would turn out all right. The World Series was resumed, and the Bay Area got down to the serious tasks of rebuilding its shattered cities.

Why do they do it? You might draw an analogy between this love affair San Franciscans have with their city and an otherwise intelligent man who risks everything: fortune, family, reputation, even health because he has fallen under the spell of some truly dazzling enchantress. In his heart, he knows it must end in heartbreak, but he feels that the time, limited as it might be, that he will spend in complete surrender to his dazzling mistress is worth the sacrifice of everything else in life.

The reasoning may be flawed, but in San Francisco it is applied on a massive scale. The City is such a seductive enchantress that it has inspired a fanatical devotion in its citizens for over a century, and is not above casting its spell on a visitor. As a turn of the century boxer once put it: "I'd rather be a broken-down lamp-post in San Francisco than the Waldorf-Astoria in New York," and many a visitor, after sampling the famous San Francisco cuisine, or topping one of its hills on a rattling cable car echoes the words of a song taken very seriously hereabouts, and leaves his heart behind when an unkind fate forces him to leave for a lesser clime.

No one can claim to have seen San Francisco without having become acquainted with the city's famous cable cars, as well-known and popular a symbol as any city has ever acquired. Started in the 1870s as a solution to climbing the horrendous grades of the city streets, they are small, almost invariably over-crowded, noisy, uncomfortable and completely lovable. Powered by a moving cable positioned in a slot some inches below the street's surface, they are moved along when a metal grip controlled by the car's operator seizes the cable. The car is pulled along the steep streets, usually with a crowd of people hanging onto its open sides, violating every conceivable safety rule and having the time of their lives. How typically San Franciscan! The grip-man, it seems, knows all his regular customers well enough to carry on a continuous banter, punctuated by the rhythmic clanging of his bell, which is supposed to

A cable car ascends the precipitous grades of California Street. Pulled along by a moving cable just beneath the street surface, cable cars are noisy, drafty, uncomfortable, and completely lovable.

Colorful, exciting and highly prosperous, San Francisco's Chinatown, the largest outside of Asia, is a top tourist attraction and an absolute must for anyone visiting "The City."

be sounded to warn traffic, but which more often than not is sounded to express his joy at being alive and in San Francisco, not necessarily in that order. The sound of that bell is music to the ears of a San Franciscan, and those hundred-year-old cars the symbol of a city unlike any other in the world, and as such, sacred.

When the San Francisco street system was first laid out, the gridlock system of streets intersecting at right angles was chosen for a large part of the city. For that reason, some of the streets march up slopes that in any other city would be considered unclimbable. It also shows that the cable car system is more than a charming anachronism: it is an useful and practical solution to an otherwise insoluble problem. Marching to the tops of those hills may help explain the shapely legs of so many native San Franciscans, and it must be admitted that the view of The City from the tops of the hills is absolutely superb and makes the climb worthwhile, but it also is fun to climb them aboard one of those rattling little cars.

The cable cars run from Van Ness to the bottom of California Street in the heart of the financial district. Although Los Angeles has been making inroads into the position once firmly held by San Francisco, The City is still a formidable financial center, home to the country's largest bank, Bank of America. This bank, which got its start as the Bank of Italy, got its biggest impetus right after the 1906 earthquake, when its chief executive officer made some highly imaginative loans out of a pushcart loaded with money salvaged from the ruins of his bank, to people who had lost everything in the disaster. The bank president defended his action by saying he had excellent collateral: the word of honor of destitute people who were determined to make a new beginning and needed only a helping hand over some very rough ground. The present prosperity of the bank is proof that the trust A.P. Giannini placed in his fellow San Franciscans was well founded, although the bank now does require a bit more collateral before it issues a loan.

San Francisco also has an active stock exchange which opens at 6 a.m. to coordinate its activities with New York's. There is a tremendous amount of money in San Francisco, not a little of which can trace its origin to the nights when the Barbary Coast was synonymous with depravity and the tolling of the fire bell summoned the citizenry to witness the justice meted out by the Committee of Twelve. The towers of the financial district soar to an impressive height and are built, supposedly, to withstand the shock that inevitably must come some day.

Evening does not signal the end of the day in San Francisco but rather the beginning of the night, which in the true tradition of The City can be the most exciting part of the whole twenty-four hours. Only a few blocks from Union Square is Chinatown, reputedly the largest Chinese community outside of Asia, and something that must be seen if our exploration of The City is to be anywhere near comprehensive. Street signs are in Chinese, the telephone booths are miniature pagodas, and blocks of stores and restaurants recreate a very passable imitation of a Chinese bazaar. The crowds are friendly, and the stores, all hawking genuine San Francisco souvenirs crafted in the busy lofts of Hong Kong have honed to a fine art the old Chinese custom of separating the tourist from his surplus dollars, and making him happy over the deal. The food there is one of the best exemplifications that the tradition of fine eating that the newly wealthy 49rs established in San Francisco is alive and well, and creating a new generation of millionaires, this time with an Oriental looking cast.

There are other night spots in San Francisco, especially in North Beach, the lineal descendant of the old Barbary Coast, where one can view just how imaginatively silicone can be utilized to modify the human body. A note to would-be Romeos: that delectable blonde you are ogling and who is ogling you in return may be as artificial as those silicone-induced curves. San Francisco's reputation as a haven for homosexuals and transvestites has been well-earned. This is probably the only city in America where an openly homosexual political candidate can be. . .and has been. . .elected. It is another example of the tolerance to different lifestyles and morals that San Francisco has shown since the days of the Gold Rush; a tolerance which some people consider a blight, and others, one more example of The City's charm. You pay your money and take your choice.

The best time to visit San Francisco is any time but summer. In summer, the infernos of the interior valleys create an updraft of warm air which, creating a partial vacuum, brings in cold air off the ocean. The result is a morning overcast that can have the tourists, dressed in clothes more appropriate to Los Angeles, shivering in their tennis togs and wondering where all that talk about San Francisco's wonderful climate originated. Visit it in late February when the street-corner flower sellers are peddling violets fresh-picked that morning, and you will begin to understand why The City's charm is so pervasive.

As befits a city with a long cultural tradition, San Francisco is sophisticated, cultured, and a haven of the arts. Museums are all over the city, and its stores stock paintings and sculptures that draw knowledgeable buyers from all over the world. The City has always done things on a grandiose scale. When we drive along 101 on Van Ness Avenue, we pass a building which in size and grandeur could easily be the state capitol: in fact, San Franciscans like to tell you its dome is higher than that of the United States capitol, and that the building is larger and grander than the state capitol in Sacramento. It is San Francisco's city hall. In Lincoln Park there is the Palace of the Legion of Honor, ostensibly built to honor the recipients of that famous medal but actually a very fine museum, replete with art and sculpture, and heavily endowed by one of San Francisco's sons who wanted to leave his mark on his beloved city. On Lombard Street, on the way to the Golden Gate Bridge we see an example of how the common man has also left his mark on the city. A cluster of buildings left over from the 1915 Pan Pacific Exposition has been extensively remodeled and preserved by the people of San Francisco as a museum of fine arts. San Franciscans are fiercely proud of their city and are willing to give it their time and money to show it off to the best advantage. Lombard Street, by the way, has another distinction, one that we can experience if we take a right turn off Van Ness and start climbing the hill. When we reach the top we are on what is often referred to as the most crooked street in the world, one whose switchbacks and corkscrew curves have been immortalized in dozens of movie chases.

While people thinking of San Francisco usually think of the cable car as its symbol, it has other symbols almost as well known, notably its two bridges. The Bay Bridge, connecting The City to Oakland was built at a bargain price during the Great Depression and completed in 1936. Four and a quarter miles long with an island in the center, it is often overshadowed by its better known companion, the Golden Gate Bridge, but it is a fantastic piece of engineering which has stood the test of time both as a utilitarian highway link and aesthetic addition to the San Francisco skyline. The Golden Gate Bridge, for a long time the world's longest suspension bridge, rears proudly over the Golden Gate, its soaring steel towers often hidden in a fog and with a surging tide tearing at its concrete footings. It is indeed a fitting symbol for The City, one we will be crossing in the right direction: the northward crossing is free.

The City has another if somewhat more dubious claim to fame: Alcatraz Island, from the Civil War to the late 1960s the most secure, most dreaded prison in the whole federal prison system. Here the toughest, most intractable convicts in the nation were put into storage and taught discipline, the hard way. It is abandoned now, but a visit to its crumbling cell blocks and dining halls with sinister clusters of gas-bombs suspended from the ceiling gives us an idea of why "Alcatraz" was a word that would blanch the face of the toughest convict. Long considered escape-proof, it relied largely on the raging currents of the Golden Gate to make an unscheduled venture off the island a one way trip to eternity.

Probably no city in the United States has a more diverse ethnic mix than San Francisco. Within city limits, we can dine in French, German, Italian, Chinese, Mexican, Japanese or Korean restaurants and the cuisine will be so authentic that we will think that we are abroad. There are sections of the city where to this day hardly a word of English is spoken, yet these are fiercely loyal San Franciscans, all part of the bubbling melting pot that gives the city a flavor of its own.

Our highway passes through this dynamic city, justly considered one of the choicest jewels strung on the thin chain that is U.S. 101. It is not a city that one can assimilate in a short visit, or a lifetime, but it is a part of Highway 101 that will live in our memories, especially if we should view it from the top of Nob Hill under the light of a full moon, or in the rays of the setting sun with the Golden Gate Bridge glowing as a light-fringed silhouette. San Francisco has a way of getting into one's blood, and somehow, once we leave it, we are never again quite the same. Maybe it is because we have left our hearts here, in the shining city by the Golden Gate.

One thing we did learn, and thoroughly. The City is never, absolutely never ever, called "Frisco."

A Silver Cloud Rolls parked in front of a fine restaurant on a precipitous street. How typically San Franciscan!

Situated at the terminus of the Powell Street cable car line, Fisherman's Wharf is not only the home of many fine seafood restaurants, but also the base for San Francisco's fishing fleet.

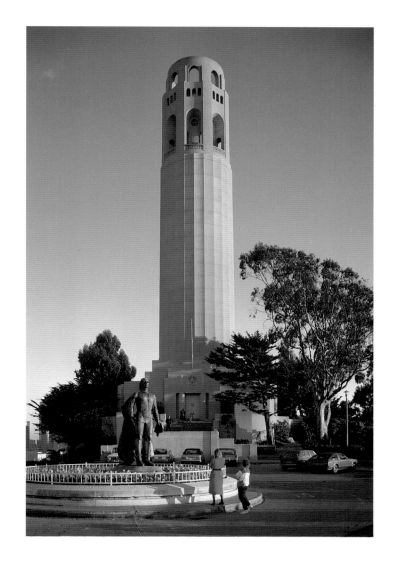

Coit Tower, atop Telegraph Hill, is a memorial to San Francisco's firemen, erected by one of their many admirers.

While most people have fond memories of San Francisco, there are a few exceptions. Among these would be former denizens of "The Rock," as the maximum security prison on Alcatraz Island in San Francisco was generally known. They'd rather just forget the place!

WINE ROAD

The only possible thing that can dull the ache in our hearts as we resolutely head northward on U.S. 101, is that the loss we feel in leaving our beautiful shining city by the bay is tempered by the knowledge that on the other side of the Golden Gate new adventures await us. We are entering a beautiful land of rolling hills, wooded mountains and a new, more relaxed way of life: ahead of us 101 leads into the Wine Country.

Travelers who have visited most of the countries of the world and are therefore in a position to make a valid judgment are practically unanimous in one particular opinion. They have noticed that the wine producing countries of the world are the lands of song and sunshine, of people who work hard, play harder, love ardently, and speed the labors of the day with a song on their lips that is an echo of the one in their hearts. They may not build many skyscrapers, but they have erected some very impressive cathedrals, and when their time on Earth is done, they leave a legacy of loving children, homes built by hard work, and bottled poetry that warms the hearts of future generations. A noble calling, indeed.

We are heading toward that kind of land as we pass over the lacework steel structure that bridges the frigid waters of the Golden Gate. We still have forty miles or so of urban development to pass before the beauties of the rolling hill country of Sonoma County are evident, but there are detours along 101 that make it possible for us to savor what is generally conceded to be the most desirable residential area of the United States. The first of these detours is onto Highway 1, our old friend from Southern California, which here is often in sight of the ocean as it winds along the headlands of the Pacific.

One of the glories of San Francisco is its proximity to so many beautiful sites, outstanding among which is Muir Woods. A mere half hour from the hustle and bustle of The City, it is the legacy of a prominent San Franciscan who bought this remote mountain valley and donated it as a national park providing that it be named after naturalist John Muir. A grove of medium-sized coastal redwoods through which Redwood Creek meanders, it is a well-tended and attended park with paved walkways that wander through a woodland that is enchanting at any time, but which, when the sun sends streamers of light through the morning mists, takes on the aspect of a fairyland. A sense of peace and serenity that somehow always seems to be associated with groves of these giant trees is very much in evidence here; possibly this was the reason that the first organizational meeting of the United Nations was held here in 1945. In such a setting, the idea that peace is worth any effort to achieve would come naturally.

Highway 1, along the coast, is very scenic, but we leave that up to your own future exploration. Since we want to see the wine country, we must return to 101, although we can take a small detour at San Rafael to visit the site of another mission.

Mission San Rafael Arcangel was founded in 1817, but the present gleaming white church was built in 1947 on the original site. This is one mission that has practically disappeared in its original form, although the city of San Rafael has grown up around it. Just one more proof that those old Franciscans picked their mission sites extremely well.

Since our objective is the wine country, we could turn off at the Napa-Vallejo exit, for this would lead us to the world-famous Sonoma and Napa valleys, sites of most of the premier wines grown in California. However, let's stay on 101 as long as possible; the charming city of Santa Rosa is just ahead and we can easily get to the wine valleys by taking detours over the hills at Santa Rosa. Before we visit these wine sites, a little background in the California wine industry might better prepare us for what we are to see in those days ahead of us. Yes, days. This is one of the most delicious bites we will be taking out of our pie, and to gulp it down would not be doing justice either to ourselves or the product. Instead, we shall savor it to the full, as befits the nobility of the vintages, both visual and liquid, that we shall be sampling.

Remember, we are still on the Mission Trail, for the last mission founded by the Franciscans is here ahead of us, in Sonoma. It is fitting that we should start our study of wine at the last mission, Mission San Francisco Solano founded in 1823, for the history of wine in California is inextricably intertwined with that of the missions.

Because wine was needed for the sacrifice of the Mass, each mission planted vineyards and made wine, thus founding California's wine industry. The grape used, the Mission grape, was not what we would consider a premium varietal grape today, but it was a prolific producer and could stand up to the treatment meted out to it by the Indians, who were, after all, only fledgling vineyardists. The fact that the grapes were crushed by spreading them out on a cowhide and stomping on them, and then squeezing the bunched-up cowhide to extract the juice may have had something to do with the sometimes gamey tang of wine made at the missions, but it was close enough to wine to meet sacramental requirements, and the chief consumers, the Indians and mission guests, had not as yet developed discriminating palates.

From this crude beginning the local industry grew. In the 1860s and 70s Count Agoston Haraszthy, a colorful Hungarian revolutionary turned winemaker imported hundreds of cuttings of varietal grapes from Europe. Some of them, their names blurred by sea water, were given imaginative names that survive to this day, Zinfandel being the prime example. Buena Vista Winery in Sonoma has the oldest stone wine cellar in the state, and carved oaken casks that have felt the hands of the legendary count.

It should be remembered that we have been seeing vineyards along 101 ever since Santa Barbara, and some even farther south at San Juan Capistrano. The Santa Ynez Valley has extensive vineyards and a well-organized group of vineyardists and winemakers whose annual celebration dinner in Solvang can be described only as awesome. The Paso Robles area has over twenty wineries, and we have already mentioned the extensive new vineyards in the Salinas Valley. There is, however, one major difference. In all these places wine was just part of a very diversified agriculture. In Sonoma, and even more so in the adjoining Napa Valley, wine is the major industry, and everything else is secondary..

Even a cursory look at the Sonoma Valley will tell you that here wine is serious business. While the vineyards are not "wall to wall" as they are in the Napa Valley, they are still extensive enough that there is no question that in this valley, the accent is decidedly vinous. Vineyards are in evidence the whole twenty-five mile length of the valley, until they merge with the extensive new plantings around Healdsburg. Tours of the tasting rooms must be taken slowly and over an extended period of time, or we may be meriting the attention of some sharp-eyed khaki-clad gentlemen driving black and white patrol cars. The courtesy of the California Highway Patrol cannot be overstated, but neither can their efficiency, both of which have been honed to near perfection by long experience in these matters.

Sonoma is a pretty little town with fine restaurants and a famous square where the Bear Flag of the California Republic was first raised on June 14, 1846, to be replaced a few weeks later by the Stars and Stripes, thus signaling the beginning of the end of Mexican domination in California. The plaza is surrounded by charming shops and restaurants and is well worth a few hours' inspection. The old mission at the northeast corner of the plaza has been completely secularized and is now a museum showing in detail the workings of a mission at the end of the Mission Trail. We should pay it an appreciative visit, and probably breathe a prayer of thanks to the men who gave us this stirring chapter of our national heritage.

The Sonoma Valley has cast its spell over many

At Newton Vineyards, overlooking the Napa Valley, terraces laboriously cut into the hillside guarantee that every available inch of soil will be utilized for the growing of the prime varietal grapes that have solidly entrenched this valley as this country's premium wine-growing region. So valuable is this land that even terracing, an admittedly expensive process, is economically justified because there is just so much Napa Valley land, and a treasure of this stature will seldom be put to any other use. The view alone from this vineyard is well worth the climb; the magnificent wine is simply a bonus.

From their backyard, Tom and Linda Burgess have this view of the Napa Valley framed in Springtime flowers. Under the morning cloudbank, the premium grapes grown there will have that exact balance of sugar and acid that guarantees not only good, but a really great wine. Blessed with the right kind of soil and climate, the Valley enjoys a lifestyle which combines hard work with the enjoyment of the fruits of that labor, so that the Valley has become one of the most sought after residential areas in the entire country.

people, from Jack London whose "Wolf House" is now a local landmark to General Vallejo, who made it one of his command posts. It got its name "Valley of the Moon" from the fact that as the moon dipped over the serrated rim of the western mountains, it appeared and disappeared several times before it set. There are a number of little towns along the way as we proceed northward, at least one of which, Agua Caliente, gives us an idea of the geothermal activity which saturates this whole area. If we follow the road as far as Santa Rosa we'll rejoin 101, but instead let's take that little side road with a sign saying "Oakville, 12 miles."

Oakville is in the Napa Valley which is one of the places we want to visit in our detour off 101. What the sign doesn't tell us is that a significant part of those twelve miles is vertical, along hairpin curves that are a sportscar driver's dream or the average driver's nightmare. The road crosses the Mayacamas Range, which separates the Sonoma and Napa Valleys and climbs to an elevation of a mile or better before, at the top of the Oakville Grade, the fabled Napa Valley spreads out before us.

The temptation to linger a week . . . or a lifetime . . . in this beautiful valley is very strong, but by now we are experts at resisting temptation, and we know it must be overcome if we are to see the rest of 101. Entering the valley at Oakville presents something of a problem: we are at the valley's midpoint and there is much to see whether we turn right or left. Another problem is that I have many friends here, a legacy of a book, *NAPA WINE COUNTRY,* that I did here a few years ago. Seeing them all is not practical: that would take a month, but there are a few that we will inevitably meet. Let's turn to the right toward the city of Napa; there is one visit we must make before we even enter the city.

For me, no visit to the Napa Valley is complete unless I visit my good friend, Brother Timothy Deiner, FSC. for over fifty years the legendary cellarmaster of the Christian Brothers Winery. On Redwood Road we turn to the right and follow the signs to Mont La Salle, the Christian Brothers' residence, school, and church. Visiting Brother Tim is obligatory in the Napa Valley, at least for myself, but the trip up there, along a winding road deep in the shade of fragrant pepperwood trees with a creek making burbling noises all the way is so beautiful that I just wanted to share it with you. This is California at its very best, and that, I promised to show to you.

The whole Napa Valley is a visual feast, a great unfenced park, with so many beautiful vistas that what would be considered outstanding anywhere else is commonplace here. Fortunately, the valley is not large, only about thirty miles long and in most places about five miles wide. Walled on either side by mountains, wooded on the western side, more rocky on the eastern, it is one solid vineyard from one end to the other, for the characteristics of the soil and climate in the valley are so perfect for the growing of varietal wine grapes that with only a very few exceptions, every inch that is not occupied by a house or a winery is planted to grapes.

There are two roads paralleling the Napa Valley, Highway 29, and the Silverado Trail, both going from Napa to Calistoga. Highway 29, on the western side, runs through a series of small towns, all of which are as familiar to wine connoisseurs as are the famous wine towns of Bordeaux or Burgundy. The Silverado Trail is still relatively untouched by urban development until one reaches Calistoga, at the head of the valley.

If there is one thing about which the inhabitants of the Napa Valley are united, it is their determination to keep Highway 29 what it is today: a crowded, mostly two-lane road that barely serves the needs of the valley, since it is usually choked with tourist traffic. A freeway, the people point out, would not alleviate the problem, but only bring more people, who are the problem. So, we must watch the traffic and break into line at the slightest opportunity, a maneuver that turns some visitors into nervous wrecks that only visits to several tasting rooms will correct. Fortunately, on Highway 29, we are never much more than a hundred yards from a tasting room.

For many years, almost all of the tasting rooms were along Highway 29, but in recent years the proliferation of wineries in the valley has been such that now the Silverado Trail, and even some of the crossroads that cut across the valley, are now studded with wineries. It would be absolutely impossible to visit every one of these in a month even if our livers were equal to the task, and we only have a few days. So, we must limit our visits, at least for this trip. This is no reflection on the ones we pass up: they're all good in the Napa Valley, or they don't survive the ferocious competition. The ones we don't visit on this trip represent a reservoir of places we

Carved oval casks, and a deep, dark cellar: in these oaken cradles, the new wines of the Sonoma Valley gently sleep in the caves of Buena Vista Winery, reputedly the oldest in California.

A new wine is much like a child in that much care and attention is necessary to bring it to maturity. At Parducci Cellars, in Ukiah, a winemaster takes a sample of the new wine for analysis.

A gondola of ripe grapes heads for the crusher. Within a week, it will be bubbling new wine, but it will be up to four years before it will be ready to release its bounty to a waiting world.

Good food plus good wine equals a good life along the Wine Road.

After a guided tour of the Robert Mondavi Winery, a tasty sip in the tasting room lends a pleasant ending to a memorable experience.

must visit on our subsequent trips: on that score, you can be very certain. Visiting the Napa Valley only once is like trying to eat just one potato chip: one taste, and we're hooked until we have seen the whole place even if it takes twenty visits. I can't think of a more pleasant addiction.

Since we must start somewhere, and we're already in Napa, let's head up-valley toward Calistoga on the Silverado Trail. A small detour takes us past the famed Silverado Country Club, home of many outstanding golf tournaments, and a wonderful place to spend a night or a month. Traveling the Silverado Trail gives us an overall view of the valley and has the added advantage of getting us accustomed to the traffic. There are new wineries along the Silverado, and most of them have tasting rooms, but let's restrain ourselves or we'll be here until we're tripping on our long gray beards. Our destination is Calistoga, but we'll make several stops en route because some of the views along the way are so enchanting that they fairly scream to be photographed.

Calistoga, at the head of the valley, is in itself an intriguing little town with a history to match. Originally called Agua Caliente from the many hot springs in the region, it supposedly received its name from Sam Brannan, a renegade Mormon who made his first stake by absconding with the tithes he had collected from the faithful. He wisely invested them in fast horses, beautiful women, and questionable business establishments, which made the enterprising young man California's first millionaire before he was thirty. During the course of the decidedly bibulous dedication of the resort he had built at Agua Caliente, he proposed a toast to "The Saratoga of California." His usually nimble tongue somewhat paralyzed by the local vintages, it came out the "Calistoga of Sarafornia". . .and the intriguing name stuck. Sam Brannan, by this time an important business man in San Francisco went on to develop Calistoga and the wine industry. I'd like to tell you more about Sam and his escapades, but I've already written that book, and there is much to see before we return to our Highway 101.

We return southward on Highway 29, past the aerie of Sterling Vineyards which is reached by an aerial tramway, and eventually arrive at Graystone, the largest stone winery in the world, which the Christian Brothers have turned into a top tasting room and tourist attraction. Let's stretch our legs here, and also take in the Charles Krug Winery, the oldest in the Napa Valley, which was first established in 1861.

We are close to St. Helena now, the wine capitol of the valley and as charming a little town as ever fought to limit its population to 5000. We pass the Rhine House, a recreation of the ancient ancestral home of the Beringer family in Germany. This place has a delightful tour featuring its famous sandstone caves hewed out of the mountainside by pickaxe-wielding Chinese coolies. We also take an appreciative look at St. Helena, a town that looks as though the first part of the twentieth century had somehow gotten stalled here, and on Spring Mountain Road we may stop to see the old Parrot Mansion, better known to devotees of the TV show as the lair of the viperish Angela Channing, owner of Falcon Crest.

The road south of town is bordered with wineries, most of which will be well-known to wine connoisseurs. There is one, though, that is practically unknown except to the discerning collector, and well worth a stop. This is opposite the beautifully landscaped Franciscan Winery, and the simple sign says "Rutherford Vintners." It's a small, inconspicuous winery, but take my word, it's worth a stop.

In the Napa Valley, small does not necessarily mean inferior, for some of the best wine is made by comparatively small wineries. Heitz Cellars, for instance, a name at whose mention the die-hard connoisseur bares his head and bows toward Rutherford, is a medium sized winery. . .by choice, and its tasting room moves a quantity of wine out of all proportion to its modest size. So it is with the small frame-house tasting room we are about to enter. The delicate Johannesburg Riesling is made in the German manner, the robust Cabernet is outstanding, and the Moscato, sold only at the winery, is so distinctive that people have been known to travel all the way from Los Angeles to acquire a single bottle. No visit to the Napa Valley is complete without adding to our wine cellar, so let's mail on the souvenirs we had accumulated for Aunt Martha and make a little trunk space for a few cases of the liquid ambrosia that, in the cold winter months, will with meditative sipping bring back memories of this gorgeous, flower bedecked valley nestled in the folds of the mountains.

Rutherford Vintners is a small, quality winery, but our next stop is at a winery that has successfully

A souvenir of California's Gold Rush, the towering overshot wheel at the Old Bale Grist Mill is part of a charming state park recalling those turbulent days.

wed quality to quantity. Probably no one in the Napa Valley has done more to popularize Napa Valley wine than Robert Mondavi, the dynamic founder of Robert Mondavi Winery at Oakville. A bundle of energy and Italian charm, this memorable man and his equally energetic wife built up a winery which is state of the art, and one which they proudly show off in one of the best tours in the valley. A feature of this winery is the Vineyard Room, with a resident chef who has evidently taken to heart the Great Chef program promoted by the winery, in which famous chefs from all over the world share their expertise. The food is fantastic; a worthy complement to the wine.

It's been a long day and we've only scratched the surface. At Yountville, let's stop for dinner. Here, Domaine Chandon has established not only a large winery making sparkling wine in the French manner, but, being thoroughly French, they have also installed a restaurant which even the discriminating French tourist, not overly prone to heap praise on American restaurants, admits is first class. The product of the winery, incidentally, is never referred to as "champagne." The French owners insist that this appellation can only be correctly applied to the sparkling wine made in the Champagne region of France. The pragmatic American, however, brought up with the idea that if it looks like a duck, walks like a duck and quacks like a duck, it is a duck, looks upon this sprightly sparkling beverage that looks, tastes, and acts like champagne and calls it what it is.

If dinner sounds too formal, we could have stopped at Sattui Winery just south of St. Helena for a snack, or more. There is a wonderful delicatessen there that has all the makings of a fine picnic lunch, and the grounds are ideal for picnicking, with an obvious source of excellent wine nearby. The Napa Valley with its Italian way of life and its appreciation of the natural symbiosis of good food and wine looks familiar to viewers of Falcon Crest as the place where the intrigue is dished up along with the food.

It is with a feeling of guilt that we must take leave of the Napa Valley, because there are so many places that we should have seen that we simply could not see in the few days that we had to spend here. Historic Inglenook, Beaulieu, the Carmelite monastery, Hans Kornell's champagne cellars, Grgich-Hill, the list is several hundred wineries long with new wineries being added by the day. Let's just say that

we've had an intriguing bite, or should we say, sip, of the Valley, and we'll come back some day to savor it at our leisure. It will be time very well spent.

Let's head back to 101 by leaving the valley at Calistoga on Highway 128, and heading toward Geyserville. The road is steep, narrow, twisting, but so absolutely beautiful that we do not mind the slow pace it necessarily entails. We top a hill and re-enter Sonoma county and Knights Valley, now undergoing development as a new wine growing region even though it has had small vineyards since the turn of the century. In a few miles, we are in the Alexander Valley.

The Alexander Valley today is what the Napa Valley was thirty years ago before the tide of vinous development engulfed it. It is first class wine land, with wines that are steadily gaining in national repute, a fact that its winemakers will tell you is a hundred years overdue. An absolutely gorgeous valley, with a backdrop of wooded mountains and well-kept Victorian mansions, it is a place that deserves a lingering look, for large areas of its natural beauty are still comparatively undeveloped in spite of the vineyards spreading like green carpets clear to the bottom of the surrounding mountains. The Russian River runs along one edge of the valley and in the summer is alive with swimmers and canoeists, all intent on escaping the pervasive heat which summer brings, and which is necessary if those precious grapes are to develop the correct sugar content.

We make a small detour off 128 to join 101 at Healdsburg, site of more wineries, past Independence Lane, where Souverain has built an imposing French chateau type winery which also features an excellent restaurant. Wine country is happy country, and that happiness finds expression not only in good wine, but also in food to match, "A day without wine," they are fond of saying in the Wine Country, "is a day without sunshine," and life is much too short to do without sunshine, drink bad wine or eat lackadaisical food.

There is no question that we are still in wine country. Everywhere there are wineries, some of them obviously new, and others just as obviously survivors of The Noble Experiment, a period which is understandably regarded in these parts, as America's Dark Ages. This area received a generous infusion of Italian blood in the 1880s, and no self respecting Italian would ever admit that anyone

A Springtime crop of flowering mustard adds a colorful note to the Napa Valley.
These plants will be plowed into the ground as a valuable green fertilizer.

On St. Helena's Main Street, the Rhine House, a copy of the ancestral Beringer home on the Mainz River, in Germany, serves as a highly decorative tasting room for the adjacent Beringer Cellars.

After a hot day of picking wine grapes, nothing tastes quite as good as a cold beer.

Floating over the Valley like an inflated inverted onion, a hot air balloon affords its happy passengers a view previously enjoyed only by the birds.

The Great Chefs program at Robert Mondavi Winery brings the world's finest chefs to the Napa Valley to share their expertise with happy students.

could make better wine than he could, with the result that there is a plethora of small wineries in the area, most of them operated by good Americans with Italian sounding names. Their colorful old buildings faithfully recreate the times when the new vineyards were planted in virgin soil, and each new vintage was regarded as a test as to whether or not a new micro-climate had been discovered.

As we approach the Mendocino County line the vineyards begin to thin out a bit, to be supplanted by grazing land supporting some very well-fed cattle. Not that we have left the wine country—far from it! At Ukiah John Parducci proudly surveys a winery that every year turns out 300,000 cases of premium wines and adds several more medals to a case already bulging with testimonials to the excellence of the wine he produces. Before 1969, he had already planted several varietal grapes that critics told him could not possibly produce good wine this far north. They were obviously wrong, for today, he is making wine from those grapes that thoroughly confounds the critics. One of my prize possessions is a bottle of 1949 Parducci Port, a souvenir of a memorable evening spent drinking the marvelous wines of this region, which I intend to drink on my hundredth birthday, when both I and the wine will have reached proper age. John attributes the excellence of his wine to the fact that he has very carefully chosen the micro-climates in which his vines flourish. These places are in evidence from north of Santa Rosa to six miles north of Ukiah.

101 winds through a series of vineyards and some wineries with impressive outputs: Italian-Swiss Colony and Weibel are both over the million case mark which should give the lie to those who say this wine country is too far north. I stopped at Fetzger, the northernmost winery on 101, and the wines I sampled there were considerably better than just respectable.

Lake county, a few miles to the right of our highway, is lately coming into its own as a wine producing county, although the roots of some of the vines are being attacked by the phylloxera beetle which decimated the wine country in the 1890s. The answer is to graft the vines to beetle-resistant roots, but that delays at least five years the production that would usually come from that vineyard. Still, more and more country north of the Sonoma County line is coming into its own as producers of fine grapes which dedicated men like John Parducci will turn into wine that is bottled poetry.

Highway 101 from the Mexican border to a point just south of Cloverdale is a minimum of four lanes of freeway, and in some places as many as eight. In this area, with a change to two-way traffic, a subtle change comes over the highway. The country is more scenic, less crowded, and for the first time on 101 we must tear our eyes from the breath-taking scenery and watch out for on-coming traffic. There is no doubt that the scenery is breath-taking: we are now in the rolling hill-country of Mendocino County, and the hills are increasingly heavily wooded. The region we are leaving behind us is undeniably fascinating and its life-style is one of the best in the whole world, but 101 passes through many fascinating areas, and the one ahead of us is unique in all the world.

The Redwood Highway beckons.

Officer Rafael Pata, whose grandfather wore this uniform as a member of the elitist Italian carabinieri, carries on the tradition by graciously posing for our camera in front of the restored Mission San Rafael.

The old swimming hole in the Russian River is a wonderful way to beat the heat of a summer day. This one is near Cloverdale.

Local legend has it that an Indian maiden, kept by parental decree and tribal custom from the brave she loved, leaped from this promontory adjacent to Highway 101 into the Russian River, hence the name "Squaw's Leap."

A slash of color on a hillside overlooking terraced vineyards, and a different view of the great unfenced park spread below rewards anyone who climbs the hill to Newton Vineyards, overlooking the central Napa Valley.

CHAPTER 6

REDWOOD HIGHWAY

While Highway 101 has taken us to some interesting places along its southern stretches, it still has not fulfilled one of the promises that was made when I first proposed we travel this highway together. The promise was of great natural beauty along the way and so far, most of the beauty we have seen has been man-made. But now, we are approaching the first of the natural wonders that have made Highway 101 a synonym for the natural splendor: the coastal redwoods and the road that winds through it, the Redwood Highway.

Anyone who has mastered the art of reading probably already knows about the redwoods, but nothing can convey the feeling of awe that these majestic trees convey except the actual sight, smell and sensation of a redwood grove. The first white men to see the redwoods and report on them were largely considered monumental liars, until the reliable Franciscans, who, in their northern missions had encountered groves of coastal redwoods, reported for once, these "liars" had been telling the unvarnished truth. It is still difficult for the human mind, without seeing them, to conceive of trees twenty feet or more in diameter and as long as a football field. It is even more difficult to describe the air of tranquillity and majesty that a grove of these awesome trees conveys. The best way to get the feeling of the redwoods is to slowly walk through them on a dewy summer morning when the rays of the early sun paint the serried ranks of the gray-brown trunks in shimmering light, and the morning mists become a glow outlining each cluster of needles with a halo of pearls. At such a time, it is

very easy to sink onto your knees, as though in a majestic arboreal cathedral, for indeed that is where you are: God lives in these trees.

My first sight of the redwoods was in 1945, when, still in a wartime uniform, I first traveled the Redwood Highway in the company of the most winsome colleen Ireland ever bred. We were on our honeymoon, and probably any place would have seemed beautiful at that time, but the fact that subsequent trips to the redwoods have only served to enhance that first impression proves that the beauty of the groves is timeless, and can only be better appreciated with repeated visits. Since then, I have traveled through the redwoods many times, and each time they become more beautiful, more inspiring, and more mysterious. This is not a simple, easily solved puzzle, but rather an intriguing mystery that becomes more fascinating as the complexity of its charm becomes more apparent with each visit. For that reason, even if I live, as I fully intend, to be a very old man, I will still find in the redwoods a source of inspiration, serenity, and renewed vigor. Because you are my guest, let me take you by the hand and show you some of the things I have learned in my forty years or so of exploring this fairyland.

As is usually the case, a little background information helps us appreciate what we are seeing. The scientific name for the coastal redwood is *Sequoia sempervirens* and with the exception of the bristlecone pine, and its cousin from the High Sierras, *Sequoia gigantea*, the world's oldest lived plant. Because of its very thick bark, high in tannin, it is virtually fire and insect proof, and when cut, its extensive root system nourishes a vigorous growth of sprouts that soon grow into trees of formidable size. Some of the trees we will be seeing are almost three thousand years old, twenty feet or more in diameter, and two hundred feet to the first limb. One of those giants, if converted to lumber, would be sufficient to build several good-sized houses, and those houses would be practically indestructible as far as the elements or insects are concerned. Your redwood picnic-table, left out in the back-yard year after year, and redwood shingles over a hundred years old are rather eloquent testimonials to this remarkable wood's resistance to the elements.

Coastal redwoods grow in a narrow belt from Southern Oregon to the Big Sur, and in isolated pockets with the right micro-climate even farther south. They thrive in a well-watered, cool climate, and so the coastal fogs of Northern California are ideal for them. In spite of all the outcry over saving the redwoods, they are hardly an endangered species. Thousands of acres of old growth giants are safely ensconced in state and federal parks, and even those on private lands are not in any immediate danger. With the exception of the imported eucalyptus, redwood is the fastest growing tree of commercial value in the United States, a fact that is very encouraging to those who want to save the spectacular old growth, and still enjoy the things that redwood does better than any other wood. Many people do not realize that the most desirable trees for lumber are not the giant old-growth trees, but those four or five feet in diameter, straight as a stretched string, that have sprung up from the stumps of trees logged over a hundred years ago. The hard economic facts are that smaller trees are easier to fall, transport, and mill, and have far less waste than those old giants. The old trees not only represent spectacular problems in moving them, but also all too often turn out to be chimneys hollowed out by fire hundreds of years ago, which the eternal redwood, with its enormous recuperative powers, has seemingly healed over. The scars are often internal, and show up only at the mill. For purely economical reasons, redwood lumber today is far more apt to come from second growth, although most major lumber companies also have large holdings in old growth trees, much of which is held in reserve as trading material for the more easily milled medium sized trees growing on public lands.

That does not mean that the "Save the Red- woods" program that had so much to do with establishing groves of these magnificent trees, which will be held in perpetuity, is in abeyance. Far from it! New groves are constantly being acquired from private ownership, and the old growth zealously guarded from its more obvious enemies. Paradoxically, some of the more spectacular groves are in danger, not from the logger, but from the people who are literally loving them to death. Compaction of the ground around these trees, caused by thousands of people walking around them in rapt admiration, is the main danger facing the giants that have withstood natural dangers for almost three thousand years.

My first trip through the redwoods, with the top down on our 1940 Packard convertible, was on a narrow road twisting between giant trees crowding to the very edge of the road, many of which had large slabs of bark missing where passing trucks had nudged but hardly stirred the gray giants. The road today is a modern four-lane freeway, but that did not come till the 1950s. A thirty-mile stretch of scenic alternate to 101—The Avenue of the Giants—is largely the old road in a slightly widened version of the same road that so enchanted us in 1945, but there are still sections of this road that reflect the problems that are endemic to its development. In some places it clings precariously to a narrow ledge blasted out of the continental shelf, with a surging ocean gnawing at its base, and at others it stands nervously on a dripping clay bank that all too often decides overnight to slide several feet downhill. The construction of this road is an epic in its own right, and while we will not have time to review all of this, a little retrospection may help us to appreciate the amount of labor it took to give us the very adequate highway over which we travel in modern comfort today.

For the first fifty years or so of settlement on the northern coast of California, little or no attention was given to a north-south road connecting the new towns of the area with the city burgeoning on San Francisco Bay. The towns of the area, Crescent City, Eureka, Arcata, and Trinidad were all sea-ports, importing their needs and exporting their products by ship. By 1855, lumbering had established itself as the premier industry of the area, and soon primitive logging railroads extended a few miles from the sea-ports. These railroads, which primarily carried logs to the busy mills also carried some freight, and

A stand of coastal redwoods near Garberville represents a scene that is almost duplicated hundreds of times in the redwood country—almost, but not quite. Each stand of these magnificent trees is different, and each has a majesty peculiar only to itself.

Against a background of evergreen needles, the pale blossoms of a flowering dogwood stand out in stark simplicity.

a few passengers long on fortitude and confirmed in their belief that they were destined to die at an advanced age, in bed. What roads there were evolved mostly in the south, toward the Bay Area, where, because of the greater concentration of population, the tax-base made construction possible. A natural extension of the road system evolved as colonization slowly extended northward, but those colonies already established in the north saw no reason to burden themselves with a road system that was neither wanted, nor at that time, needed, since all of their demands were met by ships. Actually the road system that sooner or later evolved was toward the mines and diggings in the Klamath Mountains. Communications by road between the coast and inland Redding and Red Bluff were established long before a traversable road existed between Crescent City and San Francisco.

There was another inhibiting factor. The railroads, little by little, were overcoming the formidable construction problems of the coastal route, and by preempting the most desirable site, weakened whatever impetus there was to establish on overland road. For this reason, the first crude roads connecting the coastal cities were built on the high ridges fringing the ocean, so that grades of 20% were common, and a journey of only a few miles usually entailed climbing several thousand feet up, and a corresponding distance down curves like "Devil's Elbow" and "Devil's Knee," which should give us some idea that the trip was anything but placid, even by the standards of a rough pioneer era.

It is true that as early as 1828 Jedediah Smith, following faint Indian coastal trails, had made the trip from present day Crescent City to present day Eureka, but he was a rugged mountain-man who probably could have walked across the Great Dismal Swamp barefooted had he so desired. The hard economic fact was that roads cost a lot of money, and some counties, notably Del Notre, had a rugged terrain to develop that absorbed whatever cash there was. Still, here and there, roads that had been established to haul logs to the mills were being kept open by people who had settled along them. While today those traces would probably be called goat-tracks, they were the beginnings of the system that would some day be connected into the road we call the Redwood Highway.

What travel there was in those days was through a rutted track made noisome by the long strings of pack animals that constituted the trucks of the day. A sure-footed mule can go almost anywhere, but some of those tracks were absolutely frightening, and not a few pack-strings, tied together for mutual support, ended up in tangled heaps at the bottom of some particularly precipitous part of the trail. The route presently occupied by U.S. 101 is without a doubt one of the most dangerous, challenging routes for a highway this side of the Himalayas, and a not inconsiderable part of it is stained with the blood of those who pioneered it.

The big impetus for the construction of a north-south highway came with the advent of the automobile. By this time, San Francisco was well established as the metropolis of the Pacific Coast and the advantages of an all-weather route communicating with it were apparent. For all of their dependence on ship-traffic, the northern cities were all too aware that a protracted storm could close down sea-travel for weeks at a time, and a loved-one could die in that time if denied the succor that only a large city could supply. Also, the good-roads movement that was sweeping the nation around 1909-1910 reached even into these northern hamlets so that soon a race was going on between the Iron Horse and the Tin Lizzie to see who could first get from Sausalito to Eureka.

The railroad won. In 1914, a "Sequoia Special" left Sausalito loaded down with 300 passengers who, by the time they reached Eureka were themselves pretty well loaded. Of course, they had an extra day to accomplish that pleasant task because the rail-route exhibited a tendency in whose tradition 101 follows to this day: a mud slide covered three hundred feet of track, and while it was being dug out, the passengers had plenty of time to prepare for their gala entrance into Eureka. The brazen bellow of the huge steam whistles of the lumber mills went on for quite a while; the advent to the train had been announced, appropriately enough, by smoke signals, and the mill engineers had therefore some time to work up a good head of steam.

Because the railroads had preempted the most desirable route, along the main branch of the Eel River, the new road was punched through the formidable canyon terrain of the South Fork of the Eel River, a stream which on several occasions had demonstrated that it could rise a hundred feet overnight. That, in itself, was a problem, but not the only one. The route from Garberville to Eureka lay through some of the most densely forested regions this side of the Amazon Basin. And remember, these were not ordinary trees, capable of being cut down in an hour or two by a team of tough axemen, but giants that could for days stall relay teams of axemen, first hewing an undercut in which a large man could comfortably lie down, and then cutting through the remaining wood with a twelve-foot-long "misery-whip"; a falling saw that quickly exhausted all but the toughest purveyors of Swedish Steam. There were hundreds of them to be felled if the road were to go through. Once the trees were down the problem of removing the stumps remained, and some of these were so large that one memorable one, smoothed off at the top after it was cut served for years as a communal dance floor for a remote red-wood village. The canyon reverberated for months as generous quantities of dynamite opened up the terrain to the attack of horse-drawn fresnoes and plain old pick and shovel work. It is no wonder that it took years before even a primitive route was pushed through and even more years before the road was paved so that year-round movement on it was possible. While in theory, as early as 1920 there was a road from Sausalito to Eureka, it was to be several more years before the average vehicle could master the often axle-deep mud that was more often than not the norm. Even through the late 1920s the road between Orick and Eureka was still under construction.

One of the most memorable stories from this period is that of Big Diamond, the star attraction of a circus that even in those days made regular appearances in the small towns of the timber belt, where its performances were the social event of the year and were attended by everyone able to walk into the Big Top.

Big Diamond was a bull elephant, an amiable pet of the whole circus. When the circus trucks heading toward Eureka mired down in the road construction going on north of Orick, Big Diamond's massive bulk was put to good use as he patiently pushed each heavy circus-wagon out of a series of mud holes. When the circus was once more on reasonably firm ground, Big Diamond, thoroughly exhausted, laid himself down to rest. Since the circus was ready to move, his trainer attempted to coax him to his feet, to no avail. Finally, the trainer whispered into his ear: "Show time, Big Diamond." True to the tradition that at all costs the show must go on, the huge beast tried to stagger to his feet. He couldn't make it, so he simply collapsed, and died.

Getting rid of the carcass of an eight-ton elephant posed somewhat of a problem which the circus manager rather astutely solved. He had a schedule to meet, as he pointed out to the contractor who was working on the road and there was no time to conduct funeral rites for even such a performer as Big Diamond. The hide of the dead elephant, he told the contractor, was worth between $600 and $800, and if the contractor would bury the dead elephant, the hide was his. That sounded like a fair enough propositions to the contractor who set two men to work peeling off the two-inch thick skin with axes. Weighing well over a ton, it was brought to a tannery in Eureka, where the tanner had to admit he couldn't tan an elephant hide, that contingency not having been anticipated when the tannery was built.

By this time, several days had elapsed and the skin began to do what comes naturally to untanned elephant hides: it began to emit a monumental stench. Hurriedly, the contractor had a steam shovel dig open the hole where he had deposited Big Diamond's remains, the offending skin was shoved in by a tractor-driver wearing a war-surplus gas mask, and so the elephant's bones and his hide became part of the roadbed of 101. Somewhere in our travels, we are passing over the remains of a really gallant showman.

That contractor was lucky he had steam shovels and tractors. The first work on the highway had been done by Chinese labor with picks, shovels, and horse-drawn fresnoes. In 1915 convict labor was authorized and soon up to 150 men were getting a new idea of what the "hard labor" clause in their sentence really meant as they put in long, arduous hours, six days a week, even on the days that contributed liberally to the seventy inches of rain that annually fall on this region. Strangely enough, some of the men who had completed their sentences applied for work on the project, this time as paid labor, citing previous experience on the job, and became some of the best workers on the crew. An observant foreman, how-ever, would have noticed that most of them had a marked propensity toward absenteeism on rainy days. We are traveling over a highway with a colorful history!

Much of the work in this period was in developing what had already been more or less done. The first bridges had a tendency to have been made of the local redwood, often with beams as large as 30 inches

(Overleaf) Even on an overcast day, a not uncommon occur-rence on the Pacific Coast, the littoral exhibits subtle shades of coloring that, to the discerning eye, can be absolutely fascinating.

in diameter and 60 feet long. While this may have been adequate back in the days of wagons and mule-trains, it did not quite measure up to the specifications of a modern highway, which, little by little, Highway 101 was becoming. For that reason wooden bridges were replaced with steel and concrete, and the horrendous curves and grades of the primitive road gradually improved. If any specific date for the completion of the stretch from Garberville to Eureka were to be given it would be highly questionable, because the road was in a constant state of construction until the 1950s when a four-lane freeway paralleling the old highway was finally pushed through. This at first met with fierce opposition from the conservationists intent on keeping the redwoods in as pristine a state as possible, but now that the freeway is in place, even the most determined adversary of the new highway must admit that it was done with minimal disruption to the old groves, and serves admirably to move the hordes of tourists who every year travel the Redwood Highway.

Tourists on the Redwood Highway are an old story, but back around the turn of the century, apparently were a much sturdier breed. Judge Falk, a Eureka judge with a high-wheeled Model T and an adventuresome spirit was one of the first motorists to brave the murderous grades and curves of the road in a motorized vehicle. This must have been around 1912, because it was an election year, and the judge approvingly noted that a friend of his who was running for office had posted all the more dangerous curves with election posters. Appropriately enough, his friend was running for coroner.

In the same year, Harvey Harper made the trip from Phoenix, Arizona, to Eureka over the fledgling road, with his wife and five children, one of them a babe in arms. On some of the more precipitous slopes, Mrs. Harper helped keep the car on the slippery track by hanging onto a rope attached to the car and then around any convenient tree. What made the maneuver really tricky was the fact that she had to be very careful not to snag the washtub that was lashed to the side of the car, in which the baby's things were washed out at every campsite. This region, apparently, was not settled by sissies!

Formidable as the problems were in building a road from the Mendocino line to Eureka, they paled into something approaching insignificance compared to those completing the link between Eureka and Crescent City. This latter city, founded in 1853, had been an even larger port than Eureka, serving as it did not only southern Oregon, but also the busy mines in the Klamath Mountains. It was primarily a sea-port, and its road system was confined to a few local logging traces that hardly qualified for the name of "road." As the good-roads furor spread even to remote northern California, Crescent City, the center of Del Norte County, was faced with the problem of linking up its few miles of roads with the new highway slowly pushing northward through the redwood jungles north of Orick. In an area replete with formidable obstacles, there was one that was practically insurmountable: the Klamath River. This stream, especially in the winter and spring can be a raging torrent, and while it was a bountiful supplier of fat salmon, was also too deep to ford, and too wide and swift to swim. Bridging it was the obvious solution but to a county that had many uses for whatever funds it could scrape up, that did not sound like a workable idea. Up until now, crossing the Klamath had been relatively simple: you simply waited until an Indian came along in a canoe, and hitched a ride. It is true that the ride was sometimes solicited with an extended rifle instead of an extended thumb, but the system must have been at least marginally successful, for 1800 sheep were once moved across the river in this manner. Still, it would not take the place of a bridge, and the Klamath remained a major breach in the new highway until it was bridged in the 1920s with the Douglas Memorial Bridge, presumably much to the relief of the Indians, who remembered all those sheep.

The rest of the road was equally interesting. Part of it was paved with redwood slabs imbedded into the soft earth, which was apparently quite picturesque and serviceable, but hard on wagons. A section a few miles south of Crescent City, along a precipitous slope plunging down to the Pacific, was especially difficult to maintain. The whole slope is one slippery bank of clay, and as fast as a road bed was carved out, it started slipping. Since the close-up view of the surf this engendered was not in the original plan, and no alternative route was available, the road-bed was stabilized, after a fashion, by driving long steel drill bits into the sub-soil as anchors. It helped, but even to this day, this is one section of the highway that I always pass with a certain amount of trepidation. Fresh asphalt patching along the way tells me that this section of the road is still prone to sudden drops, and it is easy to see why, in the early days of the road, this section was crossed in a state of mind ranging from acute apprehension to sheer terror.

The biggest single change in the Redwood Highway came with the opening of the Golden Gate Bridge in 1937. The end of World War I had signaled a decided change in construction methods as war surplus trucks and tractors were put to use along the highway, but the impetus given by the opening of the big bridge reached all the way up the Pacific Coast and changed the travel pattern of a nation. The Pacific Coast and the Redwoods became the travel destination of a nation increasingly mobile, and even the Great Depression could not stop some people from seeing for themselves the wonders the Save the Redwoods League had been trumpeting. Now, with the opening of a direct link to San Francisco, the trickle became a flood, and California, always a forerunner in the development of its highways, began to pay serious attention to its coastal highway system.

By this time, the various bits and pieces of what is now U.S. 101 had been organized into a federal highway. The combination of federal and state funds did what local county funds never had been able to do, and 101 became an all-weather paved road, although some sections were still narrow, crooked and dangerous. It was hardly a high-speed highway: as I recall it, even in 1945 it took three days to travel form San Francisco to Portland, most of it along 101, but they were three scenic days that I will never forget.

Enough background; let's get along with our trip. Willits is about as good a place as any to say we're on the Redwood Highway, although officially, it is called that as soon as it clears the Golden Gate Bridge. At Willits, it begins to look the way we'd expect a redwood highway to look: wooded, scenic, sometimes narrow, always interesting. Willits itself is notable as the eastern terminus of that California—and national—institution known from coast to coast as The Skunk Train.

There are two Skunk Trains, running from Willits to Ft. Bragg on the coast, along a forty mile wooded corridor that is scenic to the extreme. It was first run by a foul-smelling single car diesel train whose exhaust was so putrid that one could still smell its passage half a day later, hence its name: The Skunk. In spite of its malodorous trait, the first Skunk soon endeared itself to the people along its route. Serving isolated hamlets and ranches with an elastic schedule that was expanded or contracted as needed, it quickly became a lifeline to its customers, picking up here a housewife with a load of freshly plucked chickens destined for the hotel at Ft. Bragg or there, at the frantic waving of a red kerchief some exhausted hiker who had overestimated his ability to negotiate the heavily wooded terrain. The genial engineer would pick up a shopping list on one leg of the trip, fill it during the stop-over time, and deliver it on the way back. On at least one occasion the little train covered the distance in record time, its whistle shrieking to clear the tracks of children, tearing at top speed through accustomed stops, to beat the stork to Willits, and when it became obvious that it was a losing battle, stopping long enough for an amateur midwife to deliver an extra, non-paying passenger. It is a train with a lovable history, and deservedly popular with the people along its route who look upon it as an old friend.

The modern train has shed quite a bit of the stench, but little of the reputation. It is still a local train, consisting of four cars looking like yellow buses, but now its cargo is mainly made up of young people drawn partly by the beautiful scenery along the way, but also by the party air that pervades the train. In the summer, a separate train starts from each terminus, and at mid point in the trip, exchanges passengers, not a few of whom seem to be determined to diminish the national wine surplus, or making plans to at least go through the motions of increasing the population. It is a rollicking good time and deservedly popular, especially with excursion groups.

At Laytonville, the road becomes even more wooded, and at Piercy we see our first redwood; this one a rather scruffy object, hardly representative of the lordly specimens that are soon all around us as we enter the fringes of the redwood country. At Leggett we make a small detour to see the famous Drive-through Tree, a giant redwood that has a hole cut through it large enough to easily accommodate the average car. Naturally, we'll stop here and photograph our car with the tree straddling it like a redwood colossus. The shot is obligatory with every tourist, and we wouldn't want the operators of the resort to feel hurt if we didn't do it. We do not want to hurt anyone, especially since the peace and serenity of the redwoods is already applying its

Often overshadowed by its flamboyant competition directly across the street, this beautifully preserved Victorian mansion, the Little Carson House, is a good example of why Eureka is such a find for lovers of period architecture.

Paul Bunyon and his faithful blue ox, Babe, are immortalized at the Trees of Mystery, an imaginative and moving tour of the redwoods near Klamath.

soothing balm to our souls, and already we are becoming kinder, gentler people.

Just before we get to Garberville, we pass the famous old Benbow Inn which has been here long enough to be considered an institution. A feature of this hostelry is dining on the outdoor patio where cheeky California jays are so tame that if we're not careful, they'll fly off with our bread. Actually a delightful place to spend a few days, and soak up the peace and quiet that pervades the whole country.

A few miles past Garberville, the famed scenic alternate of 101, the Avenue of the Giants, begins. This is the old highway 101, before the four-lane freeway was put through. Do not take it if you are in a hurry, but since our purpose is to really savor the redwood country, we'll turn onto it, for this is the Redwood Highway at its very best.

If ever a road were appropriately named, this is the one. For almost thirty miles, the road winds through solid stands of giant trees, broken only by an occasional glimpse of the South Fork of the Eel River, or a small lumber community. It is a road that should be taken slowly, as befits the fact that it is narrow, deeply shadowed, and passing through forest vistas of such unimaginable beauty that it would be sacrilegious not to pay homage to them. The road is generously furnished with turn-outs, so there is no excuse for not stopping and letting the beauty and majesty of the redwoods seep into our souls.

To really get the feeling of the redwoods, one must get out of sight of the road. That is not too difficult: there are trails everywhere leading into the depths of the forest and by the time we have covered a hundred yards the sounds of the passing traffic are completely muffled by the heavy curtain of trees, and we are in a different world, completely alone with ourselves.

We sit on a forest floor that is foot-deep in fallen redwood needles, through which a thick cover of oxalis plants has pushed an emerald green carpet, and for several minutes listen intently to. . .silence. The light, filtering through a high-flung canopy of branches hundreds of feet above our heads is greenish, and, if the day should happen to be overcast, of an incredible softness. There is a softness in the air, also, mingled with the clean smell of the giant trees, and in the Spring, the delicate perfume of flowering dogwood and California bay. If it should

be a sunny day, the forest floor is a mosaic of light and shadow, as sunbeams struggle through the network of branches and throw a spotlight of brilliant color onto the forest floor, lighting it with splashes of color that only emphasize the great amount of forest that is in shadow. Then, gradually, as we willingly succumb to the beauty all around us, a sensation steals over us that is probably unique to this place and time. It is as though all the peace and quietude of the world had been poured into a vast sylvan bowl, and we are invited to drink from it to our heart's content. Drink, drink deeply, for this is one of the sublime moments of life, especially since it may return to us any time our minds should take us back to this heavenly spot, and we again feel as though we are being cradled in Nature's arms with all the affection only a lover or a loving mother can give.

There are several small villages along the Avenue of the Giants, mostly economically depressed. The great flood of December, 1964, practically wiped out the town of Weott, where the water stood twenty five feet deep on the main street of the town, and all the other towns of the area, Redcrest, Myers Flat, Pepperwood, suffered damage from which they have never recovered. This is a frequent flood plain of the Eel River, and part of the regenerative process that keeps the redwoods healthy, for a new generation of shoots poke through the newly deposited silt almost before it has dried. It is a little rough on the inhabitants, though, and explains why this unbelievably beautiful region is so sparsely settled. The main official business is harvesting second growth redwood, but the other industry, unofficial and much larger, is the clandestine cultivation of marijuana. There are isolated spots in the redwoods where, I was warned, I should not go, for the people who tend their plots in the depths of the woods are definitely anti-social, and are apt to express their feelings with automatic weapons fire. Obviously, the peace of the redwoods does not sink into everyone.

The urban center of the redwood country and the county seat of Humboldt County is Eureka, a bustling coastal city of about 25,000. In the 1880s when redwood was king and the area surrounding the city fed the hungry lumber mills, the lumber barons built their ornate homes here, and several of them are still standing; a tribute to the longevity of the redwood of which they were constructed. The most famous of these is the Carson House, now a private club, but easily viewed, at least on the outside, from a public street. A prime example of the Carpenter Gothic school of architecture, it was built by William Carson, a wealthy timber baron much respected and liked in the community, during a depression in the lumber industry, presumably to keep his men busy. It took them two years, and $75,000, a princely sum in those days, but the result is probably the most famous Victorian home in existence. The house his son built, known locally as the "Little Carson House," would be even more notable if it were not across the street from the more flamboyant parental dwelling, since it suffers considerably from the comparison.

Before we leave Eureka, we really should take in a local attraction even if it plays hob with our cholesterol levels. This is the famous Samoa Cook House, an actual old-time logging camp cook-house given a new lease on life as a top-notch tourist attraction. Breakfast is served logger style, which means it is heavy on ham, eggs, bacon, sausage, strong coffee and flapjacks swimming in pools of melted butter. We sit at a long table with perfect strangers with whom we are soon showing off the family snapshots and swapping tips on the road ahead, especially on what not to miss.

Even if our friends at the Samoa Cook House had not alerted us, I would have, for two miles north of Orick there is one of the best kept secrets in the whole length of 101, and it richly deserves to be exposed. This is Rolf's, a German restaurant on the left side of the road.

Rolf Rheinscmitt is a German-trained chef who got tired of the hassle of big city life and decided to settle in some small town where he could cook for a few discriminating clients, thus making a modest but adequate living. He especially wanted to cook the things that he had found over the years to be tasty, healthful, and inexpensive enough that he could field a menu that would not bankrupt either him or his clients. He chose Orick, formerly a busy lumber center but now much reduced in size, and established a small restaurant specializing in a menu drawn from local produce, both fauna and flora. The result was a restaurant so successful that he barely has time to go out into the surrounding forests to gather the herbs and plants he needs for his menus. His breakfasts are liable to feature salmon from the nearby Klamath River, fiddle-back fern from the

forest, and the Lord knows what else, but it is invariably delicious and such a relief from the usual unimaginative breakfast fare that stopping here rates high on my list of priorities. One taste, and we are liable to join the growing list of guests who come up from San Francisco or Los Angeles, take up residence in his motel, and spend a few idyllic days wandering the adjacent forests and working their way through the menu. That menu, by the way, were it presented in a large city, would soon make the restaurant the focus of the cognoscenti, and require reservations a month in advance. Word is getting around as it is, and getting a table for dinner without a wait is a bit chancey. I have found that if I get there around 8 a.m. Rolf is always there to surprise me with something different: elk, wild boar, buffalo, exotic fruits, or a German farmer breakfast that is substantial enough to last me for the whole day. A genuine Indian tepee on the grounds is available, presumably to take care of the surplus guests who are happily eating their way through the menu.

There! I told you I would show you some things about Highway 101 that are not generally known. Good food and good wine are one of the allowable pleasures in life, and since our trip over 101 should be enjoyable, I don't mind sharing with you the things along the way that are apt to be memorable.

Another little secret is a few miles ahead, just past the Prairie Redwoods state park. We'll get to that in time, but first let's stop and photograph one of the last remaining herd of Roosevelt elk in the state of California. More or less confined by a fence that any one of them could clear at a bound if they so desired, they are so accustomed to humans and the clicking of cameras that they don't even raise their heads as cars come to a screeching halt and the tourists pour out, cameras at the ready, to record this bit of readily observed wildlife.

Now, for our little secret. Just past the park, on the right hand side, there is a gravel road and next to it a sign saying "Cal-Barrel Road." This road is a rarity in the park system: it takes us for three miles off the main highway into some of the best redwood groves in the whole park. One of the best things about this road is that it climbs a rather steep grade, and from that grade we can photograph the trees without pointing our cameras upward and getting those converging verticals that plague so many of the pictures taken in the redwoods. The road is little used, which probably accounts for the pristine

Built in 1927 and now fully renovated, the Benbow Inn has for generations been a favorite resort on the Redwood Highway.

quality of the groves along it. Treat this place carefully, please! It is one of my favorite haunts, and I don't want to come back a few years from now and find the place knee-deep in litter.

Generally, the redwoods are beautifully kept and visually clean, except for a few privately held spots where blatant signs advertise things that strike a jarring note to the general peace and tranquillity that prevail in the forest. Souvenir shops abound, some of them perfectly in keeping with spirit of the redwoods, and so compatible, others so stridently garish that they constitute visual pollution. Somehow, this jarring note in the symphony that is the redwoods only serves to emphasize the beauty of the rest of the country, just as the beauties of the court of Louis XIV stuck a small patch on a cheek to emphasize the perfection of the face on which a foreign object was conspicuous.

We are approaching the Del Norte County line now, and the redwood groves are a solid wall, this time with no freeway to give relief from the traffic. We pass by a long beach with a roaring surf and a dangerous undertow—a beach full of mobile homes some of which stay parked here for weeks, their occupants apparently fascinated by the play of light on tumbling waters, and lulled to sleep by the roar of the surf forever planing an already firm beach.

At the top of a long hill where we look straight down to the pounding surf below us, and then swing in gentle curves through our last redwood grove, we finally descend to the beach level and Crescent City, northernmost city in California along Highway 101. The Oregon border is only a few miles ahead.

The redwoods have been quite an experience, and a fitting culmination to a trip which has taken us 944 miles from the Mexican border to the border ahead of us. We have seen Highway 101 change from a busy city freeway to a meandering country road, and the country change from a parched desert to a lush forest soaked with seventy inches of rain. We have had a love affair with a few cities and valleys, and still the road lies ahead. What can it possibly offer that we have not already seen?

We shall soon find out, for ahead of us lies Oregon, the land of sea, sand, and scenery,

Generations of tourists have posed with their cars at the Drive Through Tree, a redwood so huge that an opening large enough to accommodate the average car still leaves the tree alive and growing.

A colorful giftshop provides everything from redwood burls to souvenir backscratchers so that the wonderful trip you had through the redwoods will never be completely forgotten.

On the banks of the Klamath River, a golden bear, symbol of California, truculently guards the entrance to the redwood country.

The Russian River lures a fisherman to its banks in man's age old quest for that big one that doesn't get away.

CHAPTER 7

SEA, SAND AND SCENERY

When we first made out plans to explore U.S. 101 together, you will remember that one of the enticements held out to you was that the highway was arguably the most diversified highway in the United States. We have certainly seen a variety of terrain along its reaches, from the flat beaches and teeming cities of Southern California, its lush wine country, to the final glory that is the redwoods. The spell of the redwoods is still strong upon us as, crossing into Oregon, we leave California with the idea that no spell can be potent or long-lasting as that cast by those gigantic trees.

The redwoods admittedly are a hard act to follow. What could be more awesome or majestic as those timeless groves, with their aura of peace, tranquility, and mystery? The answer is that nothing can. The spell cast by the redwoods is unique and unlike anything else on this earth: that is the thing that makes the redwoods experience so memorable. This, however, is only one of the many faces of beauty that Highway 101 has to offer; each one is unique, and each one in turn will hold us enthralled. Simply because we have drunk deeply from the cup of beauty that the redwood offers does not mean that we have exhausted our capacity to experience other joys. Rather, the redwoods experience has sensitized us to the fact that 101 offers a variety of experiences, each one beautiful in its own right, and each one deserving to be explored and enjoyed in turn. Remember, the attachment that we had for our California cities was followed by an equally strong attraction to the wine country, and then the redwoods pushed these other memories to the back

ground of our minds. The world is full of wonders, and Highway 101 winds through more than a few of them.

Not the least of these is the famed Oregon Coast we are now approaching. While we got a small preview, along the northern coast of California, of what is to come, nothing can quite take the place of actually standing on a headland and watching a wave that got its start a few thousand miles away in the broad Pacific crash in thundering splendor against the rugged edge of the continent that is the Oregon Coast. There are other places along the Pacific Coast, the stretch from Carmel to San Luis Obispo being the best example but the accessible and highly visible indented bays and headlands of the Oregon Coast put on a display unequaled anywhere else. Highway 101 gives us a grandstand seat view of that happening.

We do not have a very long wait before we are treated to a sample of what is to come for the next few hundred miles. Just north of Brookings, the first town in Oregon, we stop for a cup of coffee in a pleasant little cafe, and just outside our window the ocean is assaulting a rocky bay in a welter of churning waters and wind-driven spray. The amount of film we shoot on just this one scene triggers a quick calculation. Hurriedly, we turn back to town and replenish our stock of film: evidently, we will be needing it in the next few miles.

Our first purchase in Oregon brings us another of the delights that abound along 101: there is no sales tax in Oregon, one of the few states in the Union where that happy condition, at least for a tourist who is not forced to pay the state income tax, prevails. Also, when we stop for gas, lured by the prices that are pleasantly competitive with neighboring California, we are politely informed when we try to serve ourselves that self-service is not allowed in Oregon, and an attendant fills our tank and cleans our windshield. Clearly we are in a state quite different not only from the one we have just left, but also from most others.

Conditions similar to those that inhibited the building of highways along the northern coast of California also prevailed here. The early settlements had a strong dependence on sea transport, since practically all of them were built at the mouths of rivers, which offered the only indentations in this rocky coast. The terrain, while it is even more steep and treacherous than the California coast, does not have the forest cover of the redwood country. Not that it is not wooded: far from that! But here, the forest growth is on a scale which, while it would seem formidable to an Easterner, is not nearly on the gargantuan scale of the forests we have encountered in the last few days. The growth here is mostly Douglas fir and hemlock, with a generous dash of spruce and deciduous trees.

The idea of a road along the coast is actually a comparatively recent one. For one thing, conditions here were even more difficult than along the California stretch of the highway, for the Oregon Coast plunges precipitously into the sea for a great part of its length, and the rain is even more pervasive than it is farther south. Added to this is the fact that a coast road would have to cross at least six major river mouths, requiring expensive bridging, and the economic base of the region was still very precarious.

As is often the case, military necessity was the catalyst that eventually spawned action. World War I had made people aware that the Pacific Coast, from the mouth of the Columbia to the Mexican border was practically undefended, and an easy avenue of invasion for a determined enemy. The Oregon Legislature voted $2,500,000 toward the cost of a military highway bordering the coast that would make possible the rapid deployment of troops in case of need. The government never met its part of the commitment, but the idea of a coastal road had been planted, and was soon incorporated into Oregon Highway Department plan of action.

It was a formidable undertaking. Whatever overland travel along the coast had ever existed had been along the packed sand of the beaches, which as early as 1913 had been declared public highways, and so removed from any chance of private ownership. Although the law was repealed, it was reinstated in 1947 in a revised form, so that to this day most of the beaches are public property. The major difficulty was that not all the coast was beaches. Some of the terrain was so formidable that the first roads wound along precipitous headlands and clung precariously to narrow ledges blasted from the edge of the continental shelf. Given such obstacles, it is understandable that it was not until 1937 that the six major rivers were bridged, and a paved road ran from Astoria to the California border. Ever since 101 was completed, it has been in a more or less constant state of relocation, rebuilding and widening, for the original road can best be described as frightening.

It is amply evident that the highway was cut through difficult terrain. Everywhere, there are enormous cuts along the ridges parallel to the ocean and vestiges of old road which has been almost entirely replaced by a broader, straighter, safer road that does a wonderful job of going from point A to point B, but which is not always as picturesque as the old highway was. In numerous places, it is possible to turn off onto the old highway and that narrow, tortuous track gives us an idea of what travel was like along the old highway.

I remember! When I first traveled this route in 1945, the narrow road twisting like a wounded snake along the edges of cliffs engendered a fear of heights in my frightened little Irish bride that persists to this day. The towns were much smaller then and the accommodations rather primitive, compared to the many comfortable motels that edge the modern highway today. The slides that were so much in evidence in a road suffering from three years of wartime neglect are still a problem, but not nearly as fearsome as those shaky stretches that we sometimes crossed saying a few very fervent prayers. The scenery, seen for the first time, was so superb that progress along the way was at a snail's pace. Every mile brought a new panorama of tumbling waves, cream-colored surf, and the sibilant sound of pebbles being rolled ashore by an advancing wave, and then brought back by a receding one. That, at least, has changed very little.

The first ten miles north of Brookings, if explored thoroughly can easily account for a full day. It would be a day well spent. Just the exercise we would get

In the Spring, Highway 101 through Oregon is alive with the colors of thousands of wild rhododendron plants. In case you may be planning to transplant some of these to the family gardens, please be advised that the alert Oregon State Police have a decidedly narrow point of view about such ideas. Better to leave them where they are and take them home in photographs.

If you had the value of the film shot every year on this one subject, you could retire as an extremely wealthy person. Probably the most photographed lighthouse in the world, Heceta Head Light stands on a promontory named for Bruno de Heceta, a Spanish explorer who, in the middle eighteenth century, made very accurate recordings of this coast.

climbing down sometimes steep trails to hidden coves and beaches would trim off some of the excess pounds we accumulated in San Francisco and the wine country, and while it may be rough on shoes, will get us to places we simply could not have seen from the road, even if we used every one of the many vista points along the way. If you are not the athletic type, you can still get a good idea of the beauty of the coast solely by using the view points conveniently located and well marked along the way; but if at all possible, I recommend you explore the hidden spots, some of them real gems of remarkable beauty. A word of caution: do this carefully and obey all common sense beach rules. Stay away from rocks jutting out into the surf, especially on windy days or during a rising tide, or you may find yourself clinging to a rocky pinnacle with the hungry waves surging at your toes. . .if you're lucky. Stay away from loose logs, especially those near the shore line: a large ''sneaker wave'' could send that log crashing down onto you, and be careful not to touch any of the jellyfish, however colorful, that abound in the tide-pools. Their poisonous tentacles can inflict a painful wound that in susceptible persons can be fatal. Wear shoes that give a good grip, even on sometimes wet rocks, and never go out of sight of other people alone. If you did have an accident and started calling for help, remember you would have some powerful competition from an indefatigably roaring surf. The coast is a beautiful siren, completely ready to enchant you with her charms, but she is also a shameless vixen who will kill you if given the chance.

The trip from Brookings to Gold Beach is apt to be a slow one—the road presents a new and enchanting scene every few hundred yards and each one demands to be admired. When we do get to Gold Beach we are tempted again, for this is at the mouth of the Rogue River, and the mail-run up the Rogue is a famous white-water adventure.

Basically, the mail-boat services the ranches and farmhouses along the Rogue River, practically all of which are accessible only by the river. It is the proud boast of the United States Postal Service that a simple postage stamp will deliver mail to any postal address in the country, which will come as somewhat of a surprise to city dwellers accustomed to having their mail go awry. Nevertheless, the service does accomplish some remarkable feats, and this is one of them. A few passengers can be carried on the run, which threads through some spectacular scenery and even more spectacular rapids. Bring your camera and wear clothes that won't be harmed by water: the trip is fun, but can get a bit wet. . .and rough.

Along the length of 101 we have passed amusement parks and exhibits, some of them worth seeing, others eminently forgettable. Fifteen miles north of Gold Beach, on the left hand side is one that possibly qualifies as the most informative and intelligently done display the whole length of the highway. It is announced by a life-sized replica of a Tyrannosaurus Rex looming above a patch of woodland tropical in its lushness. It represents the lifetime hobby of a man who, while not a professional paleontologist, probably knows more about the age of dinosaurs than most professors lecturing on the subject. This park is the expression of his hobby. A self-guided tour with concisely worded, simple language signs explains each replica of the dinosaurs which, in prehistoric times, roamed this area in incredible numbers and diversity. The replicas are life-sized, painted in realistic colors and so artfully posed in the luxuriant foliage of the rain-forest, that they look as though they are ready to leap out at us. One hour spent in this thoughtful display will teach us more about the age of dinosaurs than the average colorless college course. A sobering thought: the age of dinosaurs, the period when they were lords of the earth, lasted a hundred and fifty million years, and recent research indicates that they were anything but the sluggish reptiles they have usually been portrayed. Man, by comparison, has been on earth on somewhere near his present form for less than thirty thousand years; a mere blink in geological time. This display will not only entertain, but also instruct in a very pleasing manner.

At Port Orford, there is a spectacular view of sea-stacks—isolated rocks set out into the ocean—that are conveniently viewed from the roadside park commemorating the white man's first contact with the famed Port Orford cedar. This was on June 9, 1851, when a group of shipwrecked sailors were besieged by Indians on a large rock just at the water's edge. The sailors were the unwilling recipients of flights of beautifully crafted arrows of an amazing straightness, and to say that these made quite an impression on them is stating the fact literally. The arrows were made of a local cedar whose straight grain and strength made it admirably suited for this purpose. For decades, before synthetic materials took the place of wood, Port Orford cedar was the standard material for making top-flight arrows, and even today, some die-hard traditionalists prefer it to any other material. The wood is also used in furniture and door frames, but extensive over-logging has made the available supply very limited, and second growth is just now coming into production. Still, when the growth is achieved, Port Orford will be ready to supply the demand, and in the meantime mines the durable lode of tourism.

The whole country around here shows that it was extensively logged, then cleared and converted to grazing country. The moist, cool climate fosters a fine growth of wool on sheep, and the hills around Langlois, Denmark, and Bandon are dotted with wooly ambulating lawn-mowers who keep the pastures cropped like the lawn of an English country estate. . .which is indeed the way English estates are kept clipped.

A scenic turn-off to the left five miles before we get to Bandon takes us to Face Rock, a spectacular jumble of rocky beaches, headlands, and surging surf. This is a favorite place for storm-watchers, a phenomenon on the Pacific Coast which bears a little revelation.

Like the stormy petrel that glories in the foulest weather, the storm-watcher's idea of a good day is a fifty mile an hour wind coupled with a flood tide. No matter that such weather usually means a driving rain: the confirmed storm-watchers don their oil-skins and are out in droves, glorying in the crash and boom of giant storm-driven waves throwing spray a hundred feet into the air as they meet the rocks with a fury that is continually renewed as the rocks stubbornly refuse to be washed away. If the next day should be sunny, we can count on monumental traffic jams as thousands of watchers converge on choice spots to watch one of Nature's most spectacular demonstrations of the forces at its command.

Another thing that brings out watchers is the annual migration of the California Gray Whales from the Arctic to their breeding grounds in Baja California. These strangely graceful big mammals travel near enough to the coast that a pair of good binoculars will enable us to see them occasionally come to the surface, then in an incredibly smooth, oleaginous roll, disappear into the depths. The spouting of the whales, easily spotted from the headlands, is usually accompanied by enthusiastic shouts of "Thar she blows!" from youngsters who seem to have an intimate knowledge of whaling, probably gleaned from repeated viewings of *Moby Dick* on TV.

A feature of this part of 101 is the spate of souvenir factories all crafting articles out of myrtle-wood, which reputedly grows only in the southern coastal counties of Oregon and the Holy Land. A slow growing evergreen with a close-grained, highly lustrous wood that takes a high polish and is very suitable for a variety of articles, from gunstocks to bowls, it is a prized souvenir from this region, combining, as it does beauty with utility. Numerous small factories in the region turn out a flood of these articles and many of them will invite the visitor to view his own personal bowl being turned on a high-speed lathe. The wood must be carefully seasoned before it is worked, so that a large part of a shop's inventory is in the seasoning cabinets, making this a precarious financial enterprise. The wood, which is a protected species, is secured from loggers, who when they clear-cut an area, are always on the look-out for the prized myrtlewood which is worth several times an equal volume of the more common fir.

Not surprisingly, at Bandon, a quaint old seaport with a well-restored historical section, there is a cheese factory utilizing in a part the milk produced by those lawn mowers. This is agricultural country, although it got its start as a logging community. All the available old-growth has long since been cut off and the second growth now supports a renascent lumber industry, but increasingly, what is being recognized as the main asset of this region is being exploited and rapidly becoming the mainstay of the local economy. This is the region's natural beauty, and its natural offspring, tourism.

There is no question about the Coast having a plethora of beauty. It is everywhere, every year more and more people are discovering it, and Highway 101 is the funnel through which this flood of tourism is being poured. It is no wonder that the highway is being expanded to four lanes wherever it is possible, although some sections of it, blasted out of the cliffs of the continental shelf, will probably always remain scenic bottlenecks. The route is surpassingly beautiful, even if much of its splendor has been some-what diminished by "progress": it started with enough surplus beauty that even the somewhat tarnished remains are still extremely impressive.

Coos Bay, the largest port on the Oregon Coast

On the beach at Yachats, a little dog takes her mistress for a walk, and together they savor the golden glory of an Autumn sunset.

When the early builders of Highway 101 punched through the first rudimentary highway along the coast, they were stymied by the rugged terrain of Humbug Mountain. Even with modern technology, the road builders found it more expeditious to go around the mountain than through it or along its steep flanks.

does a thriving business in exporting logs to the small lumber mills of Japan where, using extremely thin-curved saws, they are sawed into the exacting dimensions demanded by Japanese industry. A measure of the comparative scarcity of population on the coast is that in a three hundred mile stretch, this is the largest town; its population is under twenty thousand, and most of the others are less than half that. Even so, this is a quantum jump from the population of forty years ago, when most of today's cities were mere hamlets. The Coast is being increasingly settled by newcomers whose incomes come from other regions, and who pick it as a home because, to be brutally frank, it has very few assets of its own.

Coos Bay marks the southern edge of the Dunes Country, a phenomenon which marches northward for over fifty miles. This is one of the outstanding attractions to be reached by 101 and always comes as a surprise to most people, who usually associate sand dunes with deserts. The dunes are the result of a geological oddity: an extension of the continental shelf across which the rivers of the region flow and deposit their loads of silt in comparatively shallow waters. Washed ashore by wave action, the fine sand is picked up by coastal winds and blown inland where it is deposited and sculptured into graceful dunes. Little by little, the dunes crept inland, for many years their progress unhindered, engulfing in their suffocating embrace trees whose stark white skeletons lend a eerie touch to a landscape more reminiscent of a parched desert rather than a region receiving better than forty inches of rain yearly. Recently, imported grasses have been planted to halt the march of the dunes, and today the dunes have not only been stabilized, but are actually retreating. They will never actually disappear, as long as the rivers carry silt to the sea, but probably will be more or less confined to the area they presently occupy.

Several roads penetrate the dunes, and overlooks allow us to see into a good part of the reserve, but to really see the dunes one needs a dunes buggy, a specialized four wheeled vehicle with oversized tires and a light chassis, designed to navigate in soft sand and climb the steep slopes that prevail on the leeward side of the dunes. A really surprising sight is to see three-wheeled all terrain vehicles, some of them operated by children not yet in their teens careening over the steep slopes, apparently unaware

of the fact that their chances of becoming taxpayers could be severely circumscribed, or even terminated by one wrong turn.

There are surprises awaiting us as we penetrate the dunes, not the least of which is to find veritable oases, usually around some small lake, completely hidden from view by the surrounding sand mountains. These are shelters for the surprising amount of wildlife that has adapted to life on the sandy wastes, and actually thrived there. When we explore the dunes, we shall probably see some of these animals at close range, because with the instinct that always seems to tell animals that they are in a protected reserve, they become unafraid of humans and often can be approached at quite close range. So, bring your camera, well protected from blowing sand, plenty of sunscreen, because the light reflected off the light yellow sand can induce a ferocious sunburn, and a full canteen. Marching over the dunes á la Beau Geste can bring on a fantastic thirst.

Walking all over the dunes is fine if we have unlimited time and are satisfied with seeing a comparatively limited area, but the dunes buggies are not difficult to drive and give us plenty of mobility. Several organized tours in larger versions of the dunes buggies are also available and are highly popular because the drivers know all the best places to go and are experts at scaring the wits out of the passengers without exposing them to too much danger. They are not above stopping at the top of a tall dune and letting the kids jump thirty or more feet down a precipitous face before landing in the soft sand at such a shallow angle that the contact with the sand is quite gentle. It's a wonderful playground for the young and the young at heart: I can hardly wait to get back and show those kids how to really get some distance on that dune jump.

The crown jewel of the dunes park system is Honeyman State Park, a real little gem set at the eastern edge of the dunes, with a fine campground, good swimming and a very well used picnicking area. We have been seeing good to excellent campgrounds all the way up the coast, but the stretch ahead of us, we are told is especially rich in campsites that are not only first class, but also are so beautifully situated that the problem becomes one of moving the occupants out to make room for new arrivals. People comfortably ensconced in one of those gorgeous spots have a tendency to spend the balance of their vacations right there unless politely moved out, or in a pinch, forcibly evicted.

All that exercise has developed quite an appetite, and fortunately there is a place nearby where that can be put to good use. Twenty or so years ago there was a small café some two miles north of Florence called "Maries." The food was good and little by little it grew, changed its name to the Windward Inn, and grew to be quite a large restaurant, but by some miracle managed to keep the quality that had made it prosper. Today, the town of Florence has grown out to the place, and you often need reservations for dinner. It is one of the few places I know that understands that in order for a "no smoking" area to be effective, it must be a separate room from the smokers. The food and the ambiance here—Mozart, a blazing fireplace, and a view onto a gorgeously landscaped garden is good enough to make this one of the flowers we should smell along the way, especially since this can be accomplished without inhaling a lungful of nicotine-tainted air.

As we leave Florence, we leave a coastal plain that has prevailed for several miles and once more climb onto a narrow shelf high above the ocean. Our next stop is at Sea Lions Caves, a major attraction on 101. Billed as the world's largest sea-cave, it serves as a habitat for the Steller sea lions that inhabit the coast. It is a huge hole in the ocean wall through which large waves wash, each wave apparently bearing on its crest one or more sea lions to be deposited, apparently unhurt, into the interior of a cave almost as large as a football field, and inhabited by dozens of the sea-going mammals who are as incredibly graceful in the water as they are awkward on land. This is one of their rookeries, and the cave is alive with the sharp barks of what passes for love songs among sea lions.

There are lions in the surf, also, outside the cave, and in the background, the world's most photographed lighthouse, Heceta Head Light. There are good vistas of the lighthouse, picturesquely situated on a jagged headland that is named after Bruno de Heceta, a famed Spanish explorer who would have become even more famous in history as the discoverer of the Columbia River when he made the observation in 1775, seventeen years before Robert Gray discovered the river close to the latitude and longitude entered into Heceta's log with the notation: "There is a large river in this vicinity." The huge breakers of the Columbia Bar apparently defeated his best efforts to enter the river, and cheated him out of a discovery that would have given him an even greater renown than he enjoys.

We are now in the narrowest, twistiest, and probably most scenic part of the whole length of Highway 101. For the next twenty miles it is one scenic wonder after another, each seemingly more awesome, more redolent of sheer power and violence, as mountainous gray-green walls of water rise, swell, and tumble onto themselves in a continuously repeated ballet that is never ever quite the same. Like snowflakes, no two waves are exactly alike, although they do have a pattern, and the knowledgeable observer can pretty well predict when the next really big wave will occur. This is an area with beach names often mentioning the Devil, as though this were his playground, probably as a cooler alternative to his usual clime. Cape Perpetua, Yachats, Tillicum, Waldport, Seal Rocks, all the way to Newport, the views are of beaches in sheltered cover, headlands through which the incessant waves have worn holes, and wild, tumbling waters advancing and retreating in an endless dance that is as old as the formative years of the planet.

At Newport we honor an old tradition and head for the waterfront, the Old Town, take a few snapshots of the fishing fleet at anchor, and wander over to Mo's for a bowl of their famous clam chowder, a Newport institution. For twenty miles north of Newport we see something new to us on the Oregon coast. They are called the Twenty Miracle Miles, a virtually solid wall of development reaching clear to Lincoln City, where 101 turns inland and completely changes character. We pass from one town to another with practically no break—Depoe Bay, Lincoln Beach, Gleneden Beach, Taft, and finally Lincoln City. Along the way we pass a few spouting horns, where the incoming waves compress air in a cave and blow the spume through a hole in the top of the cave forty feet into the air, drenching anyone unlucky enough to be passing at that time. It's a street of souvenir shops, art galleries, restaurants, motels, everything geared to the tourist trade which seems to be the mainstay of the economy.

If we have worked off the meal we had at Windward Inn, we are close to another fine restaurant, this one in an even more elegant setting. At Gleneden Beach we pass a large resort, Salishan, which with considerable justification dubs itself "*The* Resort on the Pacific Coast."

Ah, the joys of youth! A picnic lunch, a cheery fire, and the beauty and solitude of the Oregon Dunes. Memories are made of this.

More reminiscent of a desert than an area receiving forty inches or more of rain per year, the Oregon Dunes extend from Coos Bay to an area just north of Florence.

A dunes buggy is the easiest way to gain access to the inner dunes, where unexpected surprises, such as small oases complete with freshwater lakes, await discovery.

Updrafts engendered by sun-warmed sand make the dunes a favored place for hang gliding. Besides, if one should crashland, sand is somewhat more yielding than rocks or trees.

Salishan is large, but so artfully has the whole place been designed that it blends inconspicuously into a green, manicured landscape surrounded by a challenging 18 hole golf course. While it is the haunt of types who obviously do not worry too much about what the final tab for their stay will be, it also is the sort of place where anyone of average means can spend a few days without taking out a second mortgage on the old manse, and all this in a setting of luxury teamed with rustic charm. The dining room is a sunken lounge type place with an artfully lighted storm-twisted evergreen just outside the windows, which induces an air of dining outdoors while enjoying the comforts of a cozy indoor room. The menu runs strongly to locally obtained seafood which a prize-winning chef transforms into culinary works of art. The food is top drawer, but the crowning glory of Salishan is the wine cellar, which the genial sommelier, with only a little coaxing, will be delighted to show you. It is very possibly the largest on the West Coast, and is certainly in the running for a national rating. Northwest wines are very well represented, but the bulk of the collection runs to prestigious California and imported wines from every important winery of the world.

This is a nice place to spend the night, especially since we are at a point in Highway 101 where the road changes character. Tomorrow we shall venture upon a different kind of road, one more remote from the ocean, yet influenced by it, and we should be in a fresh frame of mind when we embark upon our new adventure.

The Oregon Coast has many faces, and each one of them is attractive, some to practically everyone at all times, others to only a few at some time: when it gets too wild and stormy for the average person, the storm-watchers revel in the wildness. On a sunny day the beaches are happy with people flying kites or just walking along the packed sand, glorying in the tangy salt air that has blown across five thousand miles of ocean to reach here. By the light of the full moon it becomes a magical place with the silver-tinged waves playing their eternal bass refrain on a hard-packed beach, and even in a fog, when shapes become ghostly and sounds are muffled and without direction, the coast has a beauty that is all its own. If we open our minds and our hearts to it, we will feel the atavistic urge that binds all of us to our ancient parent, the sea, and bless the road that brought us here. This is another facet of the gem that is 101, and our lives are richer for the experience to which it has led us, here, by the eternal sea.

At Boiler Bay, a wave driven by an onshore wind explodes fifty feet high into a welter of spray. Winter storms bring out watchers in droves.

Myrtlewood, which grows extensively in southwestern Oregon, is transformed in many workshops along Highway 101 into a myriad of useful and decorative items. Here, near Bandon, a workman crafts a seasoned block into a very handsome bowl.

The chainsaw artist has roughed out the main sculpture at this outdoor studio near Seal Rock. The deft hands of an assistant take off the rough edges and imparts that finishing touch.

Large congregations of Steller sea lions gather on the rocks near the entrance to Sea Lion Caves, a few miles north of Florence.

A very large sea cave is the winter rookery for Steller sea lions, who gather here in large groups with romance in mind. Only half a mile from Heceta Head, it is a very popular attraction.

In the glow of sunset, a logging ship prepares to take on a deck load of logs for the hungry mills of the Pacific Rim. Coos Bay is the center of log shipping on the West Coast, and annually moves impressive tonnage. This is a somewhat controversial subject since the subsidized foreign mills can pay a higher rate than local mills, thus wreaking hardship on the latter. The other side of the coin is that the foreign trade keeps a large segment of the logging community busy, and Coos Bay certainly does not suffer from the foreign money pouring into its coffers. One man's food can be the other man's poison.

A loop road south of Bandon takes one to Face Rock, a very scenic jumble of sea-stacks easily seen from accessible view points. In late Spring, the vista is considerably enhanced by the ubiquitous Gorse, whose bright yellow flowers mask a tough, thorny weed generally considered a blooming nuisance. As long as one does not have to wade through it or grub it out of one's land, it can be at least partially forgiven for the filip of beauty it imparts, especially to a seascape such as this one at Face Rock.

As the sun sets over storm-tossed waves at Lincoln City, a lonely herring gull waits for the waves to wash ashore its evening meal.

The wine cellar at Salishan Lodge is world class, with many thousands of bottles from the world's most prestigious vineyards. Yes, they'll be delighted to share their bounty with you.

Salishan is a complete resort with all kinds of outdoor sports, but its crowning glory is its challenging golf course, in a setting of transcendental beauty. Well worth a stay.

(Overleaf) Sunset on the Oregon Coast near Humbug Mountain . . . only one of the many reasons that Highway 101 has an astonishing number of repeat visitors.

CHAPTER
8

THE PASTORAL LAND

It is a well-known fact that people can experience mood changes and that these fluctuations often depend on circumstances, even though their personalities remain basically unchanged. There is a similarity between the moods of people and those of a great highway, and nowhere is that fact better demonstrated than in the change of mood that takes place on Highway 101 a few miles north of Lincoln City.

Up till now, U.S. 101 has been something of a cosmopolite, a suave sophisticate equally at home on the beaches of Southern California, enjoying the lush charms of the wine country, or exploring with enthusiasm the pleasure of the missions and the cities along its way. It has gloried in the redwoods, and the splendors of the Oregon Coast with equanimity, but here it enters a new and different phase. For the next few hundred miles, it will explore a country which is basically rural, even bucolic in feeling. It is simply another one of the many faces of Highway 101, another sign of its promised diversity, and one which in its freshness is very attractive.

Three miles north of Lincoln City, the highway, which has turned sharply inland at the city's edge, splits, and the greater part of its traffic is siphoned off on highway 18 toward Portland and Salem. For the first time in its whole length, 101 ceases to be a heavily traveled arterial and becomes a simple little country highway threading through a series of small towns. Shorn of the greater part of its traffic, it becomes quieter, as if it were enjoying the beauty of the countryside through which it meanders and in no hurry to get to any place in particular.

It is not invariably in this mood: remember this is a highway with a variety of faces, and in this region it is showing us several of them, often in the space of a few miles. Most of the time it is inland, although here and there, simply to reaffirm the idea that it is a highway under the influence of the ocean, it will give us a tantalizing glimpse of the coast, or offer a short detour that will take us to a town whose limits are washed in salt water. Still, in its lower reaches, this part of the highway does not offer the oceanic vistas that had so enthralled us in our journey along the lower Oregon coast. Instead, it offers views of wooded hillsides with old, weathered barns nestled into the folds of the hills, and numerous pastures populated with well fed cows.

The rivers of the area are numerous and invariably placid, meandering through their heavily wooded tunnels as though they were loathe to merge with the nearby ocean. Some of these ring a bell in our memories; the Nestucca, for instance.

Few travelers marveling at the "old growth" Douglas firs of the Coast Range realize that they are looking at the results of a fiery clearcut that took place way back in the 1830s, as certified by the journals of the Hudson's Bay trappers. A fire set by the Indians to clear the land, so that the undergrowth on which the game fed could grow, got out of hand near the Nestucca estuary and swept over three million acres of forest, clear up to the Columbia River. From the ashes of this catastrophe, the Nestucca Burn, the beautiful forests of today sprang, but if the Indians had not set this fire, Nature would have in time cleared the land, either through wind-

In the gentle Oregon mist so pervasive on the coast, a barn stands in a lush pasture near Hebo, looking as though it had grown there.

storm, insects, fire, or disease. Harsh, by our standards, but it is Nature's way of clearing a mature stand of vegetation to make room for the next generation.

Whatever the cause, the result is certainly beautiful, and we are reaping its benefits today. Practically all the small towns through which we pass have some forest products activity, but increasingly, as we proceed northward, the dairy industry begins to prevail. Large barns and pastures dotted with dairy cattle become prevalent from Cloverdale clear up to Tillamook.

Cloverdale bills itself as "Oregon's Best Kept Secret," and the citizens of this pretty little town can well be forgiven if they want to keep their town as it is: an enclave of old-time values that Time somehow forgot. We can stop in an old-fashioned drugstore and have not only a creamy ice cream soda that is straight out of the 1920s, but even a "Green River," a fountain drink I last shared with a freckled-faced tomboy who broke my boyish heart when I was in the fifth grade. Way back then, it cost a whole nickel, and today it costs a half dollar. At least the taste is the same.

The dairy farms become even more prevalent as we pass through beautiful pastoral country to Tillamook. Just before we reach that city, over on the right, we see two extremely large hangars that were built to house blimps that were used on submarine patrol in World War II. Today, at least one of those hangars is used to house a different kind of lighter-than-air craft: the Cyclo Crane, a revolutionary new design that can do things that not even the largest helicopter can do. The hangars are reportedly the world's largest structures built entirely of wood, a fact made necessary by the scarcity of structural steel during the war years.

Tillamook is well-known regionally, and more and more on a national scale as the home of Tillamook cheese, the product of a co-operative that was founded at the beginning of this century to find a market for the surplus mild produced by the area's many dairy farms. The answer was a cheese factory which quickly established a local, then regional, and finally national reputation for a product of such uniform excellence that it can command a premium price in the competition with the giants of the industry. Tillamook cheese has never been sold as surplus to the government food banks, even though it is eligible, if the co-operative so wished: the product is too much in demand on the open market;

a fact of which the co-operative members are quietly, but justifiably proud. Most of the dairy farms in the area sell their surplus milk to the factory, so that, with an assured year-round market, they can well afford the neat homes and well-maintained farms which give the whole area a prosperous look. The modern factory, right next to Highway 101, is a major tourist attraction with a self-guided tour that explains simply and graphically how white milk is turned into mellow yellow cheese,

North of Tillamook, the highway leans toward the ocean again and passes picturesque Garibaldi, nestled into a snug cove on Tillamook Bay. Soon we are skirting the shores of the bay, once more enjoying superb marine settings, and proceed through Wheeler and Nehalem to the promontory of Neahkanie.

The road climbs sharply to pass this sheer headland which drops steeply into the ocean. Neahkanie is the site of one of the most persistent Indian legends in the whole Northwest. Many years ago, the legend says, a great "white-winged canoe" cast anchor off the rock, and a party of men carrying a heavy chest came ashore. Hours later, the party returned to the ship, but without the chest and with two fewer men. This classic version of a pirate crew burying treasure and leaving two dead men as guardians buried atop the chest has so intrigued generations of treasure hunters that until recent legislation outlawed it, Neahkanie was becoming as honeycombed as Gibraltar. Amateur excavations all over Neahkanie were making it resemble the proverbial Swiss cheese, all to no avail. Neahkanie and its guardian ghosts have kept its secret very well, even though a new generation of treasure hunters, armed with state-of-the-art metal detectors, still carry on clandestine searches all seeking to become rich from buried pirate plunder.

The area we are now approaching constitutes another change of mood for 101, this time a reversion to the Yachats-Cape Perpetua region. There are numerous campgrounds utilizing the beautiful sites that abound, clear to the water's edge, and Arch Cape offers some glimpses of a wild, rugged littoral that persists almost all the way to Cannon Beach.

This resort city was named after an armed ship was wrecked in the area and a cannon was washed ashore. If the replicas liberally spotted along the way are a true representation of its type, it was a carronade, a short stubby cannon firing a large ball

Near Cloverdale, which bills itself as Oregon's best kept secret, a herd of dairy cattle which is the base for the region's prosperity, grazes contentedly on the lush pastures that grow year round in this mild, damp climate.

At the Tillamook County Co-operative, the rich milk produced by the region's dairy herds is made into a yellow, mellow cheese that is so good it has brought national fame to this small town. The public is invited to view this extremely interesting process which has rapidly become one of Oregon's top tourist attractions.

Quite a difference from the eight lane freeway of Southern California, but this is also Highway 101, here shown near Hamma Hamma.

The boardwalk at Seaside. Crowded in summer, relatively empty in wintertime, which is nevertheless, many people's favorite time to visit this pleasant little town.

It looks vaguely Venetian, but this is actually another face of Seaside, this time a bit inland.

Rising abruptly from the ocean floor, the promontory of Neahkanie dominates the coast north of Wheeler. Highway 101 crawls precariously over its rugged face.

at short range, but more often loaded with a variety of scrap iron and used to clear the decks of invaders. . .or mutineers. It would be interesting to find out just what kind of craft was carrying this type of armament, and if it had any possible connection to a crew that could bury two of its own along with a treasure chest.

Haystack Rock, an aptly named large sea-stack close to shore, now is so surrounded by houses all seeking to command a view of the famed landmark that it is difficult to get a good view of it from the road. We can, however, get a fine look at it by climbing down a steep bank and walking along a flat, firm beach, with a multitude of begging seagulls for company, providing, of course, that we could find a place to park the car, something that becomes more and more difficult every year as this very popular part of the coast becomes increasingly crowded.

The town of Cannon Beach is a typical resort town with most of the facilities geared to the tourists who flock here in droves, especially during the summer months, when the seaside cities are agreeably cool. This is also the entrance to one of the most famous parks on the whole coast; Ecola State Park, famous for its views of a varied and wild coast, but equally interesting because of the road leading into it. About three miles long, it is an adventure in careful driving, winding through a steep, rugged terrain generously studded with oversized Sitka spruces. Unfortunately, the road is so narrow and steep that there is barely room for one turn-out on the whole length—a pity, because the road offers scenery that should be viewed at length to be correctly appreciated.

By this time we should have worked up a good appetite, and the Crab Broiler is just ahead. This famous restaurant, at the junction of Highway 101 and Highway 26, has for years been recognized as one of the outstanding sea-food restaurants in the United States, a reputation that is well-maintained, as we soon find out as we tie on the proffered bib and vigorously attack the barbecued crab that has had not a little to do with establishing the restaurant's reputation. Why is the bib provided? Because few people have the foresight to bring their own, and to fully enjoy cracked barbecued crab one should dive into it enthusiastically, with little or no respect for the niceties of polite dining. It's a bit messy, but so delicious that no one seems to care, especially when everyone else is doing it. It is

understandably a favorite place of the kids who are right in their element when for once they can get messy to their hearts' content without getting scolded for it.

We are nearing historic country now, for ahead of us, past Seaside and Gearhart is Astoria, rich in Northwest historic lore as the site of the first American settlement in the Northwest, the mouth of the Columbia River, and the nearby site where the Lewis and Clark expedition spent the winter of 1805-1806. The site has been artfully recreated in a faithful copy of the palisaded log fort, Fort Clatsop, where the expedition spent a rainy winter plagued by rotten food, smoky and drafty quarters, and the friendliest fleas on the coast. The town of Astoria, site of John Jacob Astor's venture into the Northwest fur trade, and later the object of one of the most memorable "trades" in the annals of the Northwest, is so full of history that it richly deserves an overnight stay so that we can smell to the full one of the most delightful flowers that blooms along the long reaches of U.S. 101.

After considerable effort, Astor's men by 1811 had finally established a viable fort at Astoria so that when a party of Northwest Fur Trading Company voyageurs and traders came down the river in June, 1813, they were cordially welcomed by the Americans, many of whom were themselves Northwest Company veterans. This, in spite of the fact that the War of 1812 was raging, elsewhere that is, and the Northwesterners, being Canadian, were technically enemies. In these remote regions, that was not too important, so they were allowed to stay, but the encampment assigned to them was prudently established within range of the fort's guns. The Northwesterners had a good reason for being there. They knew that a British man o' war had been dispatched to Astoria, to either accept the surrender of the fort, or batter its walls into kindling wood with its heavy guns. The Northwesterners felt that if they could acquire the fort before the man o' war claimed it as a prize, the crew could hardly seize a fort that was occupied by friendly British subjects. Taking it by force would have been unnecessarily messy and not a little bit uncertain, so they suggested that the fort be purchased, understandably at bargain basement prices, in view of the impending takeover: the price they offered was approximately one tenth of the post's true value.

The American commander somehow found out

A forty-foot Coast Guard cutter casually knifes through a breaker on the Columbia Bar, which for a long time had a fearsome reputation as a ship's graveyard.

The wreck of the Peter Iredale, which ran aground near Astoria at the turn of the century, is a grim reminder that the ocean can be a formidable opponent.

Garibaldi is a beautifully situated little lumber and fishing village with more than its share of pleasure boats, here safely docked at its marina.

about the approaching warship and since the Northwesterners were not only stalling, but also cutting heavily into the fort's food supply, took a little decisive action. Shutting the fort's gates, thereby cutting off the food supply, and pointing his cannon with lighted matches at the ready towards the visitors' massed canoes, he suggested that the time had come to make a meaningful offer. The startled Britishers hurriedly sweetened their offer to $40,000 and a safe conduct back to New York for the Astorians. The offer, about one third the fort's true value, was reluctantly accepted.

Two weeks later, *H.M.S. Raccoon* hove into view, its gunports uncovered and the crew dreaming of prize money. When its commandant found the fort occupied by civilians—British civilians, at that—he was bitterly disappointed but went through the formality of hauling down the Northwesterners' flag and running up the Union Jack, renaming the post "Fort George" and formally claiming it as a possession of the British crown.

That turned out to be a tactical error, for the Treaty of Ghent, signed in 1815, stipulated that all territory taking during the war be returned to the former owners. That meant Fort George, which reverted to the Northwest Company. John Jacob Astor declined to pursue his claims to the post, his $40,000 having been invested in some cow pastures in mid-Manhattan, the present site of Rockefeller Center, which bid fair to be somewhat more profitable than a remote fur trading post in the far-away Northwest.

Astoria today has many souvenirs of its flamboyant past. One of these that we should visit is the Flavel House, named after a pioneer Columbia River pilot who became quite wealthy by charging a pilotage fee of ten percent of the cargo's value for safely guiding a ship over the famed Columbia Bar. It may seem exorbitant today, but in those days of minimal navigational aids, was far better than losing the ship and cargo to the murderous Bar that had defeated Bruno de Heceta, and given the mouth of the Columbia a grim reputation as a ships' graveyard. It was not until a lightship was permanently established at the mouth of the Columbia that a ship could safely consider entry, even with the help of Captain Flavel's successors. The lightship has been replaced by more modern navigational aids and is now a star attraction at the Maritime Museum where many artifacts associated with the early days of

shipping on the coast are interestingly displayed. There is still a lighthouse at Cape Disappointment, and a very active Coast Guard Station at Ilwaco, which gets frequent practice in rescuing sea-sick landlubbers who had mistakenly figured that the family outboard was adequate to master the Columbia Bar.

The professional expertise of these Coast Guard members is legendary, a fact which I was fortunate enough to check out when I took part in a routine training exercise on the Columbia Bar. The day was bright and sunshiny, "flat calm" the chief petty officer at the helm of the forty foot cutter said with a grin as he casually breasted a swell that had the boat at a forty degree angle, and felt like a high-speed elevator dropping as it ploughed into the trough of what I, at least, considered to be a respectable breaker. Thoroughly at home on the Bar, these sturdy young men and women in their practically uncapsizeable boats, are on constant call and are highly respected, especially by some unfortunate boater who has either overestimated his own ability or underestimated the Bar's capacity to dish out punishment.

Crossing the soaring four-mile long Astoria-Megler bridge, we enter Washington, the Evergreen State and the last state we will visit in our journey along the length of Highway 101. Past the famed fishing port of Ilwaco we are still in a low-lying coastal plain, but soon the road turns briefly inland along the Naselle River and then along the coast until it comes to the Willapa River, famous as the purveyor of what its admirers call the world's tastiest oysters.

We can judge this for ourselves soon, for at South Bend we make a stop to see the renowned courthouse there, and we may as well have lunch. The courthouse, built in 1910, is the seat of Pacific County and has a famous interior replete with stained glass and polished wood. It is a reflection of the dreams South Bend once had of becoming the prosperous terminus of a railroad, and many fine homes were built by people who anticipated what never happened: a large growth for the town. The homes are still there, giving South Bend an air of graciousness that befits it well.

The courthouse is only a short walk from where we parked our car, near a restaurant not incongruously called Boondocks. It is a welcome surprise to find a place of this caliber in a small town in the hinterlands, but the dining room, perched on the edge of the Willapa River is pleasantly well-appointed, and the oyster stew we ordered featuring the tasty small oysters that thrive in the nearby Willapa Bay, is absolutely the richest, creamiest nectar of the sea-gods that I have ever encountered in a long life dedicated to some very fine eating. The cook flames his oysters in a mixture of brandy and whipped cream, but he also does something else he is not divulging because that oyster stew is something that on its merits alone would get him a job at Maxim's if he ever decided to leave South Bend.

The neighboring town of Raymond is definitely a logging community; there even are two statues of loggers in a small city park. One is of the old-time axe-wielding logger, the other of his hard-hatted chain-saw-carrying contemporary. This neat little town is fiercely proud of its heritage, especially as the second growth that is just now coming to maturity since this area was logged over at the turn of the century is already providing new jobs, new opportunities, and new hope for a town steeped in the old-time traditions that first developed this country. The country between Raymond and Aberdeen is clothed in the new green of young forests, living proof that trees are America's renewable resource and that this country intends to make a good living from it.

U.S. 101 is now a two-lane country road running past marshlands on one side and young forests in various stages of rebirth on the other. It is not the most scenic part of the whole highway, but it leads to some parts that are. After all, a highway is a little bit like a marriage, and when we embark upon a journey along either one, it is for better or for worse, and whenever we hit the rough spots, we can always encourage ourselves with the idea that around the bend in the road, it will be smoother and the scenery better.

That is a safe bet, because the map says we are approaching the Olympic Peninsula, the wildest, least explored part of the contiguous United States, and Highway 101 leads us directly there.

(Overleaf) The Ecola State Park Beach is famous not only for its spectacular beauty, but also for the fact that this is one of the most variable weather sections of the Pacific Coast. If you don't like the weather, wait fifteen minutes. It is almost certain to change.

CHAPTER 9

END OF THE TRAIL

It is with mixed emotions that we approach the Olympic Peninsula, the last of the faces of beauty U.S. 101 will turn toward us as we bring our odyssey to an end. That ending is still some distance ahead of us, for Highway 101 makes an almost complete loop around the peninsula before it merges with Interstate 5 at Olympia, and that loop traverses some of the most appealing country we will see in our entire journey. It is entirely fitting that the dessert should come at the end.

101 again demonstrates its variety, for this is another one of its faces. Our trip along the Olympic highway begins at the Tri-Cities of Aberdeen, Hoquiam, and Cosmopolis, once towns whose names were synonyms for rowdiness, for even in the generally turbulent frontier days, celebrations here were tinged with violence of awesome proportions. Situated as they were on the good anchorage provided by the Chehalis River, and surrounded by some of the most beautiful old-growth fir in the world, it was only natural that they should prosper as lumber ports, exporting their product as far as China, and rebuilding San Francisco after the disastrous 1906 earthquake. There is an historical link between these towns that we are now visiting and our beautiful shining city by the bay.

From the 1880s to the 1920s, Aberdeen and Hoquiam were the quintessential lumber towns, providing as they did not only the means of producing and marketing the magnificent lumber all around them, but also purveying the relaxation that those hard-living loggers made a way of life. Many an iron-muscled young giant would labor for a month in the depths of the woods, patiently bearing back-breaking labor and primitive housing. He would be kept alive only by the dream that for one hell-roaring weekend after payday, he could go on a glorious spree in Aberdeen.

Local attorneys still speak in admiration of the logger who, brought to court on the charge that he had "broken the peace in Aberdeen on Saturday night" countered with the argument that "There ain't no peace in Aberdeen on a Saturday night, so how could I break it?" The judge saw the wisdom, or at least the humor of the frontier Solomon's argument, and let him go. The logger probably wished he had been remanded to the comparative safety of the county jail when he was met at the courthouse door by the bully-boys of the two brothels he had wrecked and the saloon keeper whose front window was somewhat the worse for wear after his unruly guest had thrown him bodily through it. Such shenanigans may have been forgiven by the municipal authorities as a normal letting off of steam, but the purveyors of the town's second and third largest industries saw it in a somewhat different light.

At least he survived, after a fashion. There were numerous others who had the misfortune to become acquainted with a saloon keeper subsequently nicknamed "Billy the Ghoul" who were not that lucky. Billy ran a waterfront saloon which extended over the tidal flats. He was an easily available "friend" to the many homeless men who thronged the area, and who occasionally took a job in the logging camps long enough to finance a good binge. Most of them could barely sign their names, and so probably did not even know that the papers they obligingly signed for Billy were insurance policies on their lives. When they disappeared a few weeks later, no one thought anything of it; the area was full of drifters and Billy always picked his victims from men with no close relatives or friends who would ask nosy questions. The insurance companies, however, became suspicious of all those policies becoming payable naming Billy as the beneficiary. An investigation revealed the remains of several dozens of the missing men whose bodies had not quite made it out to sea after they had been dropped through the trap door of Billy's saloon at the height of an ebb tide as food for the crabs. His trial and subsequent execution was a public holiday, since the count of his victims was somewhere around forty men, give or take a few. Billy had obviously been carrying on his macabre hobby for years, at first with simply robbery in mind before he hit upon the more lucrative insurance scheme, and even when he began confessing to gain a few days' respite from the hangman's noose, he was not too sure of the exact number.

It was a rough era, and what few roads existed were a match for the times. When Washington became a state in 1889, the road system was practically non-existent, and was actually more advanced in the drier eastern portion than it was in the rain-sodden western part, although the burgeoning population in that part of the state soon made roads one of the highest priorities of the fledgling state. The Highway Department struggled into existence in 1905-1906, and one of its first tasks was to put together the bits and pieces of local roads the various counties had built into some kind of a cohesive highway system. Practically all the existing roads in the western part of the state started out as logging roads designed for the simple purpose of getting logs to the mill, and so were constructed with no thought whatsoever for scenic value, and not much more for safety. Nevertheless, they were the only tracks through an otherwise solid wall of timber, and as they were little by little extended, became the basis for the rough tracks that would in time connect the remote little timber towns with the outside world.

Those remote little towns necessarily had to have a way of getting their timber to the outside world, and that was either by water if they were on the coast, or by the ubiquitous logging railroad if they were not. Some of those logging railroads performed feats of engineering that were, at least in theory, absolutely impossible, and some of the trestles and bridges they built bring shudders to the modern mind, but they worked, and because they did provide a means of transportation, however primitive, inhibited the early development of roads by decreasing the need for them.

The first clearly defined roads in the Pacific Northwest were the military roads built by the Army to connect military outposts and to provide a reliable means of moving troops and supplies. Since they were financed by the government, they were independent of local jurisdiction, and by connecting military posts that often grew into cities, provided the first connecting links in a primitive state wide road system. Parts of what in time became Highway 101 began this way, but by far the greater part was done by connecting bits and pieces of old logging skid roads.

The country through which this was done was unquestionably the toughest in the whole contiguous United States. Rainfalls in excess of 100 inches yearly was routine, and the heavy clay soils of the region retained water so tenaciously that the road was literally floated through a sea of mud. There was a reason for the narrow ten-foot width that was soon adopted as a minimum standard for the road which eventually encircled the Olympic Peninsula: it was the length of the standard corduroy log which, embedded in quantity in the quagmires of the region, eventually achieved a more or less solid footing for what passed as a road in these parts.

The rivers of the region, draining the nearby glaciers of the Olympic Mountains, were short, cold, and swift, thereby necessitating bridging. These first bridges were invariably made of the local timber, and were as invariably washed out by the spring floods until they were eventually replaced with modern steel bridges well embedded into solid bedrock. They still were of ten-foot width, as were the roads, and with the advent of the automobile, this initiated a quaint little custom. Two cars, going opposite directions, on meeting, would stop and their occupants after passing the time of day, would decide which one should back off the road into the mud. After they had passed, the car still on the road would hook a chain to the other and either pull it out, or help the driver dig it out, whichever method was the more efficacious. Strangely enough, this only

The Astoria-Megler Interstate Bridge crosses the Columbia River to the state of Washington. Over four miles in length, it is not only an impressive piece of engineering, but also a piece of architecture that blends very well into the landscape of which it is a part.

Lake Crescent, an eight-mile long aquamarine gem at the foot of Storm King Mountain, is fed by glacial streams, but it is so clean and clear that swimming in it is an absolute pleasure, once you get over the initial shock of entry.

occasionally led to bloodshed, and much more often became the beginning of some life-long friendships. We will see vestiges of this road building along our journey, for although U.S. 101 today is an entirely adequate road, it still is, in this section, the most narrow part of the whole highway, all the way up from Mexico.

At the turn of the century, there was not a section of the United States outside of Alaska that was wilder, more remote, or less developed than the Olympic Peninsula, and pushing a highway through an area this primitive was necessarily quite slow. It was not until May of 1931 that an opening ceremony was held at Kalaloch, celebrating the joining of the eastern and the western part of the highway circling the Olympic Peninsula and connecting the still lively cities of Aberdeen and Hoquiam to the lumber towns of the interior.

The towns are very sedate today, although they still export a lot of lumber, and are the beginning of the northern leg of our journey along 101. We fill up with gas, because the most marked difference between the area we are entering and those that we have left is that we will be traversing country where even houses can be thirty miles apart. The Olympic Peninsula is the least explored part of the contiguous United States, and in many of its reaches is still best described as wilderness. We will thread through it on Highway 101.

We soon see evidence of the part the forests play in the economy of the Peninsula. This land is too water-logged to be good farmland; what it does best is grow trees at an astonishing rate, and those that have not been disturbed by logging grow to a gargantuan size, especially the western cedar which likes to have its feet wet, and thrives mightily in this land of plentiful rainfall. It is most unfortunate, at least visually, that cedar, with its heavy oil and resin content, is so resistant to decay, because the detritus from a cedar operation is heavy and in places, frightfully ugly. We see it on both sides of the highway, intermittently, all the way up the western side of the peninsula. It is supposed to be burned, but that is an operation that costs considerable money in this land of heavy rain, and many of the property owners, intent on wringing every cent possible from their lands, elect not to get rid of the detritus. The result is that an operation even five years old can still look like a World War I battlefield after a heavy barrage. Burning is mandatory on state

and federal lands and these quickly become clothed in the green of new forests, sometimes planted to the desirable Douglas fir, and at others allowed to re-seed naturally to the region's dominant hemlock or cedar.

Whenever we are not passing a recently logged area, the road winds through a narrow tunnel of greenery, a veritable wall of trees. Traffic is usually quite sparse, for this is relatively unsettled country and what traffic there is leans largely to heavily loaded logging trucks. In the summer, traffic picks up somewhat, for this is the way of the Olympic National Park, one of the nation's largest and most spectacularly endowed parks. . .and one of the least visited.

There are several good reasons for this. Olympic National Park is not for everyone, but it has devotees whose attachment to it borders on the fanatical. Situated as it is in the far corner of the country, well away from population centers, and with comparatively primitive accommodations, its appeal is mostly to outdoor types. Most of the park's 900,000 plus acres are in jagged, snow-covered mountains, massive glaciers, and wilderness fastnesses so wild and remote that only a very few people are physically able to penetrate them. For the average person, it remains an inaccessible, primitive land, that for all practical purposes, might just as well simply not exist. The outdoor types who glory in this kind of country love it passionately, but there are not enough of them to make the park one of the better-used recreational areas.

There are several roads leading a short way into the back country and hardy back-packers can go quite a bit farther, but this elitist group is only a small part of the people who would visit the interior were it possible to reach it more easily. The heavily laden clouds coming in from the Pacific meet the Olympic mountains, and even though these mountains are of modest elevation in comparison to the towering Cascades, they have a snow-fall out of all proportion to their height. The approach to Mt. Olympus should be attempted only by expert mountaineers and the miles of glacial seracs that must by traversed make this the most difficult climb in the whole Northwest. One of the results of this heavy precipitation at lower altitudes is the Quinault Rain Forest.

The Olympic Peninsula has several rain forests, and of these my personal favorite is the one bordering on the Quinault River. It is not as developed as the Hoh forest, but in its very wildness lies its allurement. We turn off on the South Shore Road at Lake Quinault and soon we are in sight of Lake Quinault Lodge, a venerable old structure whose gem-green lawn is a splash of color in the surrounding somber forests. Nearby is a forest walk that in an easy mile-long hike takes us through groves of Douglas firs so large that we could be back, at least in spirit, in the redwoods.

This area gets over a hundred inches of rain in the average year, and this generous precipitation fosters a tree growth that is nothing short of amazing. It also is the reason for the heavy growth of moss that gives the region its own peculiar character. Alders and maples grow to proportions here that are unheard of anywhere else, and their hoary trunks are upholstered in mats of green moss. The air is so laden with moisture captured by this absorbent tree covering that even on a sunshiny day, a fine mist is constantly falling, or at least so it seems, so oppressive is the heavy air. The mosses are a very effective sound dampener so that sounds are muffled, and even if we should be lucky enough to spot a herd of Roosevelt elk which inhabits the depths of the rain forest, their passage would be soundless as a procession of gray ghosts. The light is greenish, eerie, and in the summer, struggling to push through the mass of vegetation that is almost heavier on the branches of the giant trees than it is on the ground. Almost, but not quite, for the forest floor is waist high in ferns, mosses, lichens, fungi, and tiny flowers, all busily decaying the plentiful vegetation into rich soil. The soil is so saturated that each step is as though you were stepping into a huge green, and very wet sponge.

When sunlight does manage to struggle through the thick canopy, its rays usually shine through a fine drizzle, its path clearly discernible through the suspended droplets. The effect is dazzling, but infrequent, for more often than not the forest is clad in a semi-darkness that adds considerably to its mystery, and lacking the sublime majesty of the taller trees. In the redwoods I have always felt as though I were in God's cathedral; in the rain forest, I feel as though I were trespassing in a druid's grove, and it would not be too surprising to see a troll or two pop out from behind a moss-covered trunk.

The road ends at a campground some twenty miles or so from the main road, and in the summer it is a very well frequented place. There are no formal trails through this rain forest and the heavy, water-soaked spongy terrain, discourages walking very far into the woods unless you thrive on wet feet and soaked clothes. The ecology of the rain forest, in spite of its lushness, is quite fragile; another reason to respect it, because it is an aspect of the area that is beautiful, and deserves to be protected. The way back to 101 can be pleasantly varied by taking the first gravel road over the river and following that along the north shore of Lake Quinault. A deep, dark, cold lake this is attractive in its pristine purity, even though it is too cold for comfortable swimming. If you are a fisherman, however, look around and get accustomed to the scenery, because if you go to Heaven this is where you are liable to wind up.

Once we leave Lake Quinault, we are on the Quinault Indian Reservation, one of several on the peninsula. The road is a narrow tunnel through the trees and continues that way until we reach the ocean at Queets. At Kalaloch, there is a wildly spectacular beach, with Destruction Island on the horizon. From the road, this island appears barren with only a lighthouse breaking the low silhouette. Examination with binoculars shows it to be quite nicely wooded with a snug bay at its north end: a likely spot to pick up wood and water, back in the days of sail. At least, that's what Bodega y Quadra, a Spanish explorer who landed a party of men on this island thought. They were promptly butchered by the warlike Hoh Indians. Sadly, Quadra sailed on after naming the island "Isla de Dolores." In 1787 Captain Barkley, commanding the H.M.S. Imperial Eagle landed a party of six men at the mouth of a nearby river, and apparently the Indians' dispositions had not improved a bit, for these men met the same fate. Barkley named the river "Destruction River," but the Island has since been renamed "Destruction Island" while the river regained its Indian name, the Hoh.

A marked detour takes us up the valley of this river toward the Hoh Rain Forest and the celebrated Hall of Mosses Trail. Unlike the Quinault Rain Forest, this one is well developed, with paved trails leading to a spectacular display of moss-hung maples. In spite of the modern developments, the woodlands feeling of the area has been very well retained and the people in wheelchairs who can enjoy this area certainly appreciate the efforts that make this natural wonder available to those not vigorous enough to penetrate a primitive environment. It is

No one celebrates the Fourth of July more enthusiastically than the logging town of Forks, on the Olympic Peninsula. The whole town gets into the act, even the children, one of whom is here showing off her fancy face painting job.

It is generally conceded in the Northwest and Alaska that the very best grilled salmon is done over a bed of alder wood coals. That's the way the Forks' Lions prepare their salmon for the Fourth of July Celebration, and they never have any leftovers.

At a Crane Creek logging operation, on the Olympic Peninsula, a mammoth old western cedar had grown to such gargantuan proportions that even though it was a "chimney," it weighed more than the loader customarily used to load a log truck. It took the greater part of a day to load that old brute, using the complete leverage of the metal spar tree. Over twenty feet in diameter at its massive butt end, it was more the proportions common to a redwood, but graphically illustrates what proportions trees exposed to the generous precipitation of the Olympic Peninsula can achieve. This tree was over fourteen hundred years old, and was cut on Indian land.

Loaded onto the most massive log truck available, the log was securely braced, and with the truck in its lowest compound gear, proceeded very slowly toward a railroad siding, where two gigantic log-loaders strained in vain to get it onto a railroad gondola. After working for the greater part of a day, the crew gave up and dynamited the monster, much to the disgust of the woods crew who had worked so hard to get it to the railroad in one piece. The pieces weighed an aggregate of sixty-eight thousand pounds of usable wood. A lumber company economist with a flair for figures calculated that the company could have saved over a thousand dollars by bypassing the tree, but regulations and the contract stipulated that the area must be cleared. The lumber business is not necessarily all profit.

at this place that we hear once more a persistent legend that we have been hearing in various versions all over the peninsula. It is the legend of the Iron Man of the Hoh, and in one respect, all the different versions agree: he was quite a man!

Although there is quite a discrepancy as to the exact period that the Iron Man haunted the Hoh Rain Forest, there at least is uniformity in two aspects of his description: he hated clothes, and he was possibly the strongest man who ever lived in this region, and remember, this region is the home of loggers not exactly noted for being puny. Winter or summer, the Iron Man's attire consisted of a ragged pair of cut-offs and a waist length beard. As for his strength, of which he apparently was quite unaware, the stories are legion. No one knows for sure whence he came, although one version of the legend makes him out to be a World War I veteran severely gassed in the last months of the war, and supposedly destined for a lingering death. He had come to this region because, as an avid outdoorsman he hated hospitals, preferring to live out his last days as far away from civilization as he possibly could get. That's the upper reaches of the Hoh Valley, without a doubt.

There, he waited for the death that should have come to him in a few months. Instead, maybe because of the rugged conditions under which he lived, he made a miraculous recovery, and soon reports began filtering back to civilization of a mysterious figure haunting the rain forest, and scaring the living daylights out of anyone catching even a fleeting glimpse of him as he flitted soundlessly through the moss-draped groves. Although the Park Service looks askance at anyone establishing unauthorized residence within park limits, they were never able to find his cabin, although it is evident that he must have cashed his disability checks somewhere, and he did have a few modern conveniences.

One favorite story and the most persistent, is that of a backpacker, deep in the woods following an almost imperceptible trail, who met the Iron Man on a wintry day. Clad only in his cut-offs, with his beard wrapped around his neck for padding, he was carrying a full-sized cook-stove on his massive back. In the course of the short conversation that ensued, the hiker said: "Gosh, isn't that thing awfully heavy?" The Iron Man shrugged, "Aw," he said, "it ain't that bad, but that hundred pound sack of flour flapping around in the oven does make it kinda clumsy."

Even though the Iron Man of the Hoh was quite reclusive, his other attributes would have made him right at home in Forks, the commercial and social center of the Western Olympic Peninsula. If ever a town were to be picked as the quintessential logging town, that town would be Forks. This is the home of the brash, proud, unreconstructed logger, with all the faults and virtues of that remarkable breed. Forks lives off logging, is home to the logger, and thrives on the logger's code: work hard, play just as hard, and look out for your buddy. It also is a reflection of this spirit that makes the Forks Lions Club, man for man, the most generous, most productive club in the state, not excluding the big cities. If a project that falls within the organization's goals needs doing, and it's too tough for anyone else, that's the kind of project the Forks Lions Club will take on and ram through, come hell or high water. . .and have a rousing time doing it!

A good example of this is the Fourth of July Celebration sponsored not only by the Lions, but, in the true spirit of small town togetherness, practically every other civic organization in town. It is a beehive of activity, with dances, parades, patriotic speeches, floats with lots of pretty girls, and topped off with an Independence Day salmon barbecue and demolition derby that is a passable replica of a Los Angeles Freeway pile-up. For days, the town is jammed with visitors, for the word has gotten around that no place, but **no place** celebrates Independence Day as they do in Forks.

Naturally, this would also draw some people whose ides of a celebration would not run to dances, parades or patriotic speeches. One such group was a gang of big city bikers who, hearing of the good times to be had at the Forks celebration, decided to interject their own particular brand of terror into the festivities. Word got to Forks ahead of them, and when their parade of snarling bikes roared into town, they were met with a phalanx of logging trucks loaded with testosterone-soaked young men wielding peaveys as though they were toothpicks, and holding at arm's length chain-saws that easily outsnarled the bikes. The thoroughly cowed bikers decided to get stoned anywhere else but Forks. To them, that town was down-right anti-social. As for myself, I knew there was something about that town I liked the very first time I saw it!

Forks feeds mostly off the timber in the nearby Olympic National Forest, and is the center of logging activity for the whole western edge of the Olympic Peninsula. A road off to the left leads to the fishing village of La Push which has some nice sea-stacks, and fronts on the wildest coast line in the contiguous United States. For forty miles along the coast, there are no roads, but a hardy hiker with the right attitude and permission from the Indians over whose lands he will be trespassing can come away with once in a lifetime experience. It is no trip for a beginner, but the hiker will be rewarded with scenery little changed since the first Spanish explorer set foot on this coast.

Heading back to our highway, we find another one of those short roads giving us a tantalizing glimpse into the interior of the peninsula. This one goes along the Soleduck River, through arrow-straight second growth to a resort twelve miles up the road. The Soleduck River is generally very cold, feeding as it does off the glaciers in the interior, but it does have a few local hot-spots, which are gratefully utilized by the youngsters in the vicinity as swimming holes. The holes are warmed by the numerous geothermal springs rising in the vicinity, some of which rise in the river bed and warm the holes very agreeably.

A practical adaptation of this geothermal feature is the Soleduck Hot Springs Resort. The central feature is a series of circular pools, each with ramps leading down into progressively deeper water, with temperatures ranging from 90° to 104°. An Olympic sized pool with water at the usual 70° seems absolutely frigid after a soaking of a few minutes in the agreeably warm water of the other pools, which reputedly have all the therapeutic value of the fancy European spas, without the attendant fancy prices. Cottages are available, and some people happily roost here for weeks, "taking the waters" as they say in England. The area around it, deep in the heart of the woods, is as enchanting as any in the whole park, and is amply provided with hiking trails suited to any degree of activity. The resort stays open year round, and one of the more popular pastimes is relaxing comfortably in a pool of warm water while in winter, an occasional snowflake flutters down to give an agreeable contrast to the comfort in which the customer is lolling.

The main road, Highway 101, is as straight as a well-stretched string, sometimes for such a distance that the twin walls of trees fencing in the road on either side merge into the distance. The trees are so tall that the tops seem to converge and we seem to be traveling through a solid tunnel of verdure, opening once in a while to give us a tantalizing glimpse of a snowy mountain peak or an azure mountain lake. Just think, this is an extension of that same dusty road over which the Franciscan friars once trudged on sandaled feet, but that was long ago and fourteen hundred miles away.

The largest of the lakes in the area is at the foot of the Storm King Mountain and is an eight-mile-long crescent shaped gem from which it draws its name: Crescent Lake. The road hugs the edge of the lake, which is of a beauty that would ordinarily command an appreciative look. It is being somewhat ignored because of the logging trucks, all of which seem to be making up lost time on this serpentine stretch of road flagged at thirty five miles per hour. The way those drivers wheel their monstrous chargers around those curves in a display of driving virtuosity is something that would be admirable in a driving contest, but is apt to instill a feeling verging on panic in the average driver not accustomed to having thirty tons of steel and logs bellowing thirty feet behind him at sixty miles an hour.

It really would be nice to admire the lake, which is certainly one of the most memorable sights the whole length of the highway. Coming off the surrounding mountain peaks, the water is clear and cold, but not too cold for an appreciative swim. The East Beach turn-off leads to a nice conventional beach, but to really enjoy this lake, you should take the road from the south side of the lake to the western side, which is comparatively uninhabited. In some tree-shaded cove with the sun sparkling on crystal-clear water, shed your inhibitions along with your clothes and revel in water that embraces your unencumbered body like a cool satin sheet. This is swimming the way God intended a person to swim!

In just a few miles, we reach a stretch of ocean and there, just over the strait, the mountains of Canada's Vancouver Island climb into the sky. We have reached the northernmost point of our journey that started in Mexico, and from now on, our road will head first in an easterly direction, and then, for the first time, in a southerly direction. It will seem strange, but it still is 101, and part of our journey. We are nearing the end, but 101 still has a few more vistas to offer and a few more hills to climb.

The heavy precipitation of the Olympic Rain Forest fosters the growth of mosses that retain water to such a degree that even on days when it is not raining, a constant drizzle seeps down from the masses of sodden vegetation. The growth engendered by this generous precipitation and mild climate is absolutely astounding. This scene is on the Quinault River, about eighteen miles off Highway 101.

Hood Canal, an arm of Puget Sound, parallels Highway 101 for nearly forty miles, and affords some of the most enchanting scenery along the whole length of the highway.

Following the strait, we come to Port Angeles, the largest city on the Olympic Peninsula, and the economic center of the whole region. It is a pleasant little city, like most of the cities of the region a lumber exporting port, and geared to the tourism which has already become a sustaining part of the economy, as increasingly, the natural beauty of the region is being recognized as a marketable asset.

We make an eighteen-mile detour here for a side-trip into the hills along one of the roads that penetrates the Olympic National Park to at least the edge of this mountainous wilderness. This route is different in that it lets us see into the heart of the Park by leading us to a ridge 6000 feet above the sea, easily visible in the distance, and gives us a wonderful view of the park's interior.

Hurricane Ridge is usually open the year round, although winter snows of up to ten feet in depth often pose maintenance problems in a winter of heavy precipitation. The winding road climbs at a gentle but steady angle so that by the time we reach the Interpretive Center at the top of the ridge, we have climbed over a mile vertically, and can see a mass of jumbled icy peaks and deep wooded canyons that constitute the heart of one of the wildest, least visited, and largest national parks in the whole park system. At over 900,000 acres, Olympic National Park can hardly be considered a small piece of real estate, but less than a tenth of that area is easily accessible by car. The rest is wilderness, kept forever in a pristine state so that generations yet unborn may someday see what the whole peninsula looked like before humans and the progress they bring moved in.

Returning to 101, we head eastward toward Sequim and another one of the oddities that seem to abound along the length of 101: the Sequim rain-shadow. Here, in the lee of the Olympic Mountains, the usual 140 inches of rain common to the Olympic Peninsula dwindles to a sparse 15, and irrigation is necessary for some crops. The happy inhabitants are not complaining: the sunshine that drenches the narrow belt of country where this meteorological oddity is evident has made this one of the state's most desirable retirement spots, so that the valley is rapidly filling up with golf courses, fancy homes, and all the aspects of a resort city, while only fifteen miles away less fortunate people are sloshing around in the rain.

Sequim is also home to Olympic Game Farm where many animals routinely used in movies and TV are trained and housed. If that big bear we see contentedly sunning himself outside his snug den looks familiar, it is for a good reason: that's Gentle Ben, star of a TV show, and only one of the several furry thespians in residence, willing to perform for room and board. A drive through feature of the park allows us to photograph the park's many exotic inhabitants, but stay in your car. Some of those good-natured animals are awfully big and strong, and like most actors, can be quite temperamental.

Our next detour off 101 is at Highway 20, and it leads not only to a charming town, but also backward in time for a century or so. That is the best frame of mind in which to visit Port Townsend, a place which, in the 1880s rivaled Seattle as a lumber-shipping port, and was so important that it even had resident foreign consuls. The ornate Victorian mansions which the prosperous inhabitants of the town built are still there, on the bluffs overlooking the town, most of them converted to bed and breakfast houses and still exuding the Victorian charm that makes this little city one of the most pleasant places to visit. . .or live. . .in the whole state. Of special interest is the ornate Jefferson County Courthouse, built in the glory days before the timber ran out and the twentieth century caught up to Port Townsend. A walk around town will show us dozens of absolutely gorgeous Victorian homes, invariably very well preserved, and epitomizing all the dreams that somehow did not quite materialize.

Port Townsend is at the entrance to Puget Sound, but when we get back to 101 we will be following a scenic arm of that body of water. Hood Canal is a fish-hook-shaped salt-water arm of the main sound and provides scenic beaches, gorgeous vistas, and some of the most succulent oysters in the Northwest. We get a good example of this at the Timber House, a picturesque log-built restaurant two miles south of Quilcene. Flawed only by the fact that smoking is allowed in the main dining room, it is a beautifully appointed restaurant that exploits the plentiful seafood of the region. This is a culinary oasis on a largely gastronomic desert, for while there are good restaurants in Sequim, Port Angeles, and Port Townsend, the rest of the eating establishments along Hood Canal seem to be more dedicated to providing basic needs than a sybaritic experience.

Other than that, the trip down Hood Canal is really idyllic. The road is narrow, in the summer a tunnel of maples and alders winding by a shore line that is often a scenic feast. The towns scattered along its length are small and occasionally offer entrances to the eastern side of the Olympic National Park. One of these entrances, at Hoodsport leads to the Staircase region, along the way affording tempting views of Lake Cushman, an impoundment leading to the very edges of the rugged Olympics. In its upper reaches, it is well within the boundaries of the Park, and the temptation to explore this frigid gem of a lake is so strong that it can be satisfied only by yielding to it. Not on this trip, however, for this one is by car, and those regions are accessible only by boat, but this music of the future is much too seductive to be ignored, and I do have a Klepper kayak...

We are approaching Shelton, the last town we will visit along 101. A scenic overlook at the south end of town gives us a good view of one of the Northwest's largest lumber and plywood mills. Sol Simpson began operations here in the 1890s and ever since then, this busy mill has been feeding off a large patch of timber on the Olympic Peninsula that is on a perpetual regeneration cycle. By the time the loggers complete the loop around the area, the regrowth is ready for a second round of harvesting. This, plus extensive private holdings and a vigorous research program aimed at finding even more uses for wood in a modern age pretty well guarantees that this mill will be here for as long as wood is needed.

Highway 101 has now become a four lane freeway again, and all too soon we will begin to see signs that our rural highway is about to see another change, this time back to the busy freeway that was its initial form. At a curve in the freeway, we see a lake at the left, and above the lake, the soaring dome of the Washington state capitol. The coupe de grâce is a small sign affixed to the by now familiar 101 sign. The sign says, simply "101 end." U.S. 101 merges with Interstate 5 and we have reached our journey's end.

It has been quite an odyssey, from the arid plains of extreme Southern California to the rain-drenched mountains of the Olympic Peninsula, and in between we have seen some of the most superb scenes this or any other country has to offer. It has been a voyage of exploration and discovery, and if we are saddened at the thought that we have reached the end of our journey, we also can rejoice that we have been handed a golden key which, properly used, will unlock our minds to the further treasures that lie in such profusion along the far flung reaches that began with the El Camino Real.

The nicest part of the whole trip is the thought that now that we know the way, it can be traveled again, and again...and again.

U.S. 101. End.

(101)

From Port Angeles, a winding road leads to an elevation of over six thousand feet at Hurricane Ridge, from which an excellent view into the interior of Olympic National Park may be attained.

The Starret House in Port Townsend is one of the many fine Victorian homes liberally studded throughout this charming old seaport town.

The beautifully restored N.D. Hill Building, built during Port Townsend's halcyon days, is a feature of downtown.

On the northwest coast of the Olympic Peninsula, travelers are treated to the spectacular ocean vista known as Kalaloch Beach.

(Overleaf) Into the heart of Olympic National Park, the view from Hurricane Ridge can be either gorgeous or disappointing, according to the weather. It seldom is completely clear because of the natural pollution exuded by conifers, which changes the light to the blue end of the spectrum. The effect, however, can be enchanting.

Come fair weather or foul, the log trucks must go through if the hungry mills and loggers' children are to be fed. Here, near Forks in April, a log truck slogs through a bit of sloppy weather. It's all in a day's work.

In the shadow of the Washington State capitol dome, on a wet, drizzly day, Highway 101 rejoins Interstate 5, and completes its long journey from the Mexican border. End of the trail.

PHOTO DATA

Photographing something as varied as a long, complex highway would necessarily entail the use of some highly versatile photographic equipment, and for that reason, if for no other, the 35mm format was my first choice. The job would entail much travel, and occasionally some very rough usage, so that portability and toughness became matters of primary consideration. Here, again, the 35mm format excels, for any format that more or less withstood the rigors of photographing a book on modern logging should be equal to the task of photographing a highway that could be traveled in comparative comfort, or so, at least, I thought. That was before I ran into salt spray, blowing sand, and thirty foot waves, all of which I experienced while doing this book.

It is a high tribute to the toughness and high quality built into the professional Nikon system that the four camera bodies I used on this job survived in reasonably good shape. They needed cleaning, of course, and salt spray does weird and not so wonderful things to a camera's interior, but they are still running and ready for my next foray into the photographic jungle.

Cameras used were two Nikon F2s, and two old but completely functional FTNs which refuse to wear out. The oldest body was reserved for photos where it would be exposed to salt water, with the idea that if the camera did become a casualty, it was already depreciated out. It did get soaked with salt water, not only once, but several times, but that tough old Nikon doesn't know it's supposed to be ruined and keeps right on delivering superb quality. All exposures, unless otherwise specified were on Kodachrome 25, a film with fantastic accutance, and which delivers the quality upon which my picky-pecky publisher insists. To get deeper color saturation, my Kodachrome 25 was usually rated at ASA 32.

Lenses used, all Nikkors, were:

20mm f3.5	85mm f1.8
24mm f2.8	105mm f2.5
28mm f2.0	135mm f3.5
35mm f2.0	180mm f2.5
35mm 2.8 P.C.	200mm f4.0
50mm f1.4	300mm f4.5
50mm f2.0	43-80mm f3.5 Zoom
55mm f3.5 Macro	80-200mm f4.5 Zoom

All lenses were capped with skylight 1A filters. Exposures were usually according to the camera meters, but in case of doubt were checked with a hand held Gossen Luna Pro meter. In cases of extreme doubt, exposures were made on the basis of my eye and forty years of photographic experience.

Page	Shutter Speed	Aperture	Lens	Comments
Cover	1/250	f5.6	85mm	High overcast
2	1/30	f16	50mm f2	Tripod
6	1/125	f5.6	50mm f1.4	Courtesy U.S. Coast Guard
6	1/125	f11	35mm f2	El Camino Real
6	30 sec.	f3.5	20mm	City of the Angels
6	1/250	f4	50mm f2	Mission Trail
6	1/125	f5.6	28mm	Baghdad by the Bay
7	1/125	f5.6	50mm f1.4	Wine Road
7	8 sec.	f5.6	50mm f2	Redwood Highway, tripod.
7	1/15	f4.5	300mm	Sea, Sand, and Scenery. Tripod
7	1/60	f4	35mm f2	Pastoral Land. Raining.
7	1/125	f8	85mm	End of the Trail
10	1/250	f8	50mm f2	
11	1/250	f8	105mm	
14	1/15	f11	43-80mm	Zoom set at 65mm
15	8 sec.	f5.6	50mm f1.4	85B filter to warm up greenish light of the redwoods.
17 top	1/125	f4	50mm f1.4	Warm sunset light
17 bot.	1/125	f8	35mm f2	
20	1/250	f8	135mm	Shot surreptitiously!
24-25	1/60	f5.6	35mm f2	Pola screen
28 top	1/60	f5.6	20mm	
28 bot.	1/125	f5.6	105mm	Late afternoon light
29 top	1/125	f8	55mm macro	
29 bot.	1/250	f11	50mm f1.4	
32 top	1/500	f8	300mm	Kodachrome 64
32 bot.	1/250	f8	105mm	
34	1/250	f11	50mm f1.4	
35	1/125	f5.6	24mm	Deliberately overexposed, otherwise we would have had a silhouette.

Page	Shutter Speed	Aperture	Lens	Comments
38 top	1/125	f8	50mm f2	
38 bot.	1/125	f11	50mm f2	
39 top	1/15	f2	28mm	Available museum light
39 bot.	1/125	f8	50mm f2	
42	1/125	f11	24mm	
43	1/125	f5.6	35mm f2	
46	1/125	f5.6	50	Heavy overcast. Overexposed
47	1/250	f8	105mm	
49	1 sec.	f4	35mm P.C.	Tripod
52	1/60	f11	50mm f2	
53 top	15 sec.	f8	50mm f1.4	Tripod. Lens occasionally covered during exposure to eliminate people.
53 bot.	4 sec.	f5.6	28mm	Tripod, and Kodachrome 64
56-57	1/125	f8	35mm f2	One hour wait to get a shot without traffic.
60 top	1/60	f11	50mm f1.4	
60 bot.	1/60	f5.6	50mm f1.4	Heavy overcast
61	1/250	f11	35mm f2	
64	1/125	f5.6	50mm f2	
66-67	12 min.	f5.6	35mm f2	Double exposure. Tripod
70	1/125	f8	43-80 Zoom	
71	1/125	f5.6	35mm f2	
74 top	1/125	f4	24mm	Shot from a moving cable car
74 bot.	1/125	f5.6	50mm f1.4	
75 top	1/30	f4	35mm P.C.	Pola screen, tripod
75 bot.	1/250	f8	135mm	Kodachrome II
78	1/250	f11	50mm f1.4	Kodachrome 64
79	1/30	f16	28mm f2	Tripod
81	1 sec.	f8	28mm f2	Tripod
82 top	1/60	f4	50mm f1.4	Flash, held high and to one side. Set at 1/8 power.
82 bot.	1/60	f4	35mm f2	Light rain
83 top	1/15	f4	200mm	One weak halogen lamp, strictly to provide highlights
83 bot.	1/4	f1.4	50mm f1.4	Hand held, between heartbeats!
85	1/30	f5.6	50mm f1.4	Polarized, to darken shadows
87	1/125	f8	35mm f2	
88-89	1/30	f5.6	35mm P.C.	Polarized and tripod
90 top	1/125	f5.6	50mm f1.4	
90 bot.	1/250	f8	80-200mm	Zoom set at 200mm
91	1/30	f2.8	50mm f2	
93	1/125	f8	35mm f2	
94	1/250	f8	55mm macro	
95	1/250	f8	35mm f2	Kodachrome 64
96-97	1/250	f11	35mm f2	Kodachrome 64
100	2 sec.	f5.6	50mm f2	
101	1/15	f3.5	35mm f2	
104-105	1/125	f4	50mm f1.4	
108	1/125	f5.6	35mm f2	
109	1/250	f5.6	35mm f2	
112	1/125	f8	50mm f1.4	
114 top	1/125	f5.6	50mm f2	
114 bot.	1/125	f5.6	85mm	
115 top	1/125	f5.6	105mm	
115 bot.	1/250	f5.6	50mm f1.4	
118	1/60	f5.6	55mm macro	
119	1/125	f4	35mm f2	Pola Screen
122	1/125	f4	85mm	
123	1/60	f4	50mm f1.4	Raining
126 top	1/125	f5.6	35mm f2	
126 bot.	1/60	f11	50mm f1.4	
127 top	1/500	f4	105mm	
127 bot.	1/250	f5.6	85mm	
129	1/250	f5.6	43-80 Zoom	set at 80mm
130 top	1/30	f4	50mm f1.4	
130 bot.	1/60	f5.6	50mm f2	Weak flash fill
131 top	1/250	f4.5	300mm	
131 bot.	7 sec.	f2.8	28mm f2	Camera braced against screen
132	1/60	f4	50mm f2	Slanting early evening light
133	1/125	f8	35mm f2	
134	1/15	f4.5	300mm	Tripod
135 top	8 sec.	f5.6	28mm f2	Tripod, and a very steady model
135 bot.	1/125	f8	50mm f1.4	
136-137	1/60	f5.6	50mm f1.4	Tripod
139	1/30	f4	35mm f2	Light rain
141 top	1/125	f5.6	105mm	
141 bot.	1/15	f4	28mm f2	Kodachrome 64
142	1/60	f5.6	50mm f2	
143 top	1/125	f4	50mm f2	
143 bot.	1/125	f5.6	50mm f2	
144	1/125	f4	85mm	Heavy overcast
146	1/250	f4.5	80-200mm	Zoom set at 200mm
147 top	1/60	f4	50mm f1.4	
147 bot.	1/125	f8	50mm f2	
150-151	1/125	f5.6	50mm f1.4	Overcast
154	1/125	f5.6	50mm f2	
155	1/125	f5.6	50mm f2	
158 top	1/125	f4	50mm f2	Heavy overcast and rain
158 bot.	1/60	f4	50mm f2	Weak fill flash
159 top	1/60	f4	35mm f2	Light rain
159 bot.	1/60	f4	50mm f1.4	Light rain
162	1/15	f4	35mm f2	Self timer, tripod and 82B
163	1/125	f5.6	50mm f1.4	
166	1/250	f4	105mm	
167 top	1/125	f5.6	35mm P.C.	
167 bot.	1/125	f5.6	35mm P.C.	
170-171	1/125	f4	105mm	No filter, to emphasize natural blue haze
174	1/60	f4	50mm f1.4	
175	1/60	f4	85mm	With an informal assist from the Washington State Patrol